PRAISE FOR *THE WIM HOF METHOD*

'Wim Hof has inspired millions of people to use just their bodies
and breath to heat, then heal, themselves of a laundry list of chronic
illnesses. Dubious, you say? I certainly thought so, until I discovered
the real scientific research from real scientists around the world
proving these 'impossible' claims were in fact true. This book is a
valuable guide to anyone looking to take better control of the health,
heat, and untapped potential locked away within us all'

JAMES NESTOR

'I enjoyed this book immensely! Get inside the mind of Wim Hof
and learn why millions of people worldwide feel the freeze and do it
anyway. Breathe in, chill out, and enjoy the ride'

PATRICK MCKEOWN

'Wim Hof's program has become an essential part of my daily regimen
for self-care and grounding. I warmly recommend it'

GABOR MATÉ

'This book fortifies that the mind is the most powerful tool
we possess, however very few use it like Mr Wim Hof. A positive
and persuasive read'

ANT MIDDLETON

'Thor-like and potent ... Wim has radioactive charisma'

RUSSELL BRAND

'Wim is a legend of the power ice has to heal and empower'

BEAR GRYLLS

'This book will change your life'

BEN FOGLE

'A fascinating look at Wim's incredible life and method'

FEARNE COTTON

THE
WIM
HOF
METHOD

ALSO BY WIM HOF

Becoming the Iceman (with Justin Rosales)
De Top Bereiken Is Je Angst Overwinnen (Dutch)
Klimmen in Stilte (Dutch)
The Way of the Iceman (with Koen De Jong)

WIM HOF

THE

WIM HOF

METHOD

**Activate Your Potential,
Transcend Your Limits**

1

Rider, an imprint of Ebury Publishing,
20 Vauxhall Bridge Road,
London SW1V 2SA

Rider is part of the Penguin Random House group of companies
whose addresses can be found at global.penguinrandomhouse.com

Penguin
Random House
UK

First published in Great Britain by Rider in 2020
Published in the United States by Sounds True, Inc. Louisville, CO 80027
www.penguin.co.uk

A CIP catalogue record for this book is available from the British Library

ISBN 9781846046292

Printed and bound in Great Britain by Clays Ltd, Elcograf S.p.A.

Penguin Random House is committed to a sustainable future for our business, our readers and our planet. This book is made from Forest Stewardship Council® certified paper.

I dedicate this book to my children, your children,
your mothers and fathers, brothers and sisters.
But most of all, I dedicate it to YOU.
The YOU that resides beyond fear,
The YOU who is willing to dive deep.
My hope is for you to regain your personal power, help others,
and ultimately lend your hand to Mother Nature herself.

What lies behind us, and what lies before us are
but tiny matters compared to what lies within us.
And when we bring what lies within us
out into the world, miracles happen.

HENRY STANLEY HASKINS

CONTENTS

FOREWORD
AN UNLIKELY MEETING

BY ELISSA EPEL, PHD

t was an unlikely place for a somewhat conservative medical school researcher to be: a
business-oriented wellness conference in Palm
Beach, Florida. I wondered if I should have come, and I reminded
myself to be open—that you never know what the world has in store
for you, who you might meet, what you might learn. And then, my
reason for being there was unveiled. There he was, walking up to
the podium, wearing a T-shirt when most were in suits, a beard that
implied "I have better things to do than spend time on a manicured
trim." Wim Hof told us part of his story. He led us through the breathing part of his method. And I was absolutely struck.

What he described of his experience was exactly what I had
been searching for—ways to increase hormetic stress in our bodies.
Theoretically, a stressful exposure can have harmful effects at high
doses, but at low doses it can actually create changes in our body that
make us healthier and stronger—that's what we call "hormetic stress."
Stress researchers like me spend a lot of time exploring the dark side
of stress, how chronic stress and depression wear us down, shorten our
telomeres, and contribute to disease. But we also know that stress can
be a good thing. Acute short-term stress can lead to powerful positive

changes in our cells. Heating up a worm just a bit, for example, can increase the life of that worm, although too much heat and it becomes a funeral. Studies on hormetic stress in humans are scarce, leaving many questions unanswered. Are there natural ways to safely unlock the positive effects of stress in our cells? Do we already hold the keys to our own well-being? Where do we start the search for those answers? It seemed to me, hearing him speak, that Wim Hof had created a good map for us to explore.

After the talk, a couple approached me, Victor and Lynne Brick. Victor, having tragically lost his brother to mental illness, was looking for ways to support research on natural methods to prevent or even cure depression and other serious mental health issues. (Despite the many antidepressant medication ads on TV, several meta-analyses suggest Big Pharma solutions do not have benefits beyond the placebo effect.) From that meeting, a study was born.

When I returned to University of California, San Francisco, and told my colleagues about Wim Hof and his method, I didn't exactly jump to, "Can we study the Iceman?" That's the first thing you might have learned about him: his nickname. In the many documentaries about Wim, you see people practicing the method in small circles with him. You can feel their adrenaline and group cohesiveness, fueled by exercising the limits of their body's regulation, exposing themselves in shorts to the ice—maybe during a cold Poland winter—while heating up their bodies with their mindset and breathing method. You see people doing push-ups while holding their breath, more push-ups than they thought they could do. You see young people flocking to him, especially men, high-performance machismo in the air. You hear accounts of miraculous cures from people with disease who practice the method. All these are red flags for conscientious medical school researchers. But the potential of unleashing novel potent hormetic stress effects overrode the alarm of extraordinary claims, the skeptical reaction to his growing popularity. My colleagues saw the potential, just like I did. To our delight, Wim Hof was 100% supportive of our rigorously controlled trial.

With the fame that comes with breaking twenty-six world records, and the documentaries and popular books that feature him, Wim knows the limits of anecdote, of story, to giving a method validity in the medical world. He knows that the research path—slow, painstaking, and with the necessary attitude of objectivity and skepticism—is the only path to understanding and applying this method to health care. Research can help us unveil the method's mechanisms, document safety and efficacy, and determine in controlled clinical trials how it affects people with disease states. The method has been tested in small pilot studies so far, showing improvement of the immune system response to endotoxin[1] and in inflammatory arthritis of the spine, suggesting that it can reduce chronic inflammation and symptoms.[2] It is being tested in people with spinal cord injuries who cannot easily activate their autonomic and cardiovascular systems with exercise. It is being practiced among the elderly, with some members of the Wim Hof Method practice group over ninety years old. Wim knows that rigorous research is the path that will lead to discoveries that give more people control over their health and well-being.

I have been following the emerging peer-reviewed research on the Wim Hof Method closely. My conclusion is that we need more serious examination of this method, as it has unique potential for improving health and slowing the aging process. In our study at the University of California Department of Psychiatry, we have spent the last year teaching people with high levels of life stress the Wim Hof Method and closely examining how it impacts their daily emotional reactivity, autonomic stress reactivity, and cellular indicators of aging. We don't mention his name or label the method, because that would invoke what we call a "guru" effect—a strong belief about the method—that we could not match in the other conditions we are studying (exercise, meditation). The trial is expected to be completed this year.

This is the beginning of a new field. We already know some specific things about the method, such as how the breathing method can temporarily change the pH of our blood. The method has inspired many theories of how it works. But what we think the mechanisms are today may change over time with more research. I am so excited to learn more, for the benefit of us all, and for the much-needed shift of health care toward self-care.

The truly remarkable story here is Wim's own, as revealed in these pages. It is not a search for fame that drove Wim to accomplish feats such as swimming more than 100 feet under the ice of a frozen lake or hiking with a group to the top of Mount Kilimanjaro in twenty-eight hours. But these feats speak volumes. They show the method can push us past our assumed limits, that we can unlock the vast potential of our bodies and minds. The true story is of one man's passion, his love for nature, for all living beings, for his family, for humanity, and thus his drive to share what he now knows to hopefully heal sickness. (As a boy, he felt deeply connected to nature, so much so that he stopped eating animals at thirteen years old, completely on his own, in a culture of omnivores.) It's also a story of human suffering and striving—the humanizing experiences and insatiable curiosity that drove Wim to explore the limits of mind and body.

The true story is that Wim has shown us what we all can do. The underlying method requires something uniquely human—the power of belief in ourselves, the power of strong intention combined with directed attention. The unique dialectical state of relaxing into physical discomfort and pain—of ice, of cold water, of breath-holding—I find this to be a remarkable state. As someone who loves meditation, I believe it is an especially interesting state from which to observe the mind. It is different from sitting meditation alone—it has sharp, acute effects, demanding our full attention and interoception. Training the mind and body in this way seems to have great potential for developing stress resiliency.

The method shows clearly that what we believe determines how much we can do. As Wim points out, "Whether you think you can or you think you can't, you are right." The research group from Radboud University in the Netherlands, led by Dr. Kox and Dr. Pickkers, published a study showing that optimistic outcome expectancies are associated with some of the physiological responses to the method.[3] The method requires engagement of body and mind, and at least some belief.

I am so glad I attended that meeting in Palm Beach. I am honored to introduce you to Wim Hof and what may be one of our big revolutions in health and self-care, our ability to apply and self-prescribe our own levels of hormetic stress. The next generation of answers lies in science. I remind myself, and you, that science is a slow process of incremental knowledge building where no one study proves anything. We should look very carefully at this method, and those derived from it, with both safe self-experimentation and rigorous scientific inquiry. I therefore suggest that you suspend any automatic judgments of disbelief and, rather, turn toward your curiosity and openness. Allow yourself to experience the Wim Hof Method in your own body and make your own discoveries. Enjoy!

PREFACE

IT'S ALL THERE FOR YOU

Would you like to have more energy, less stress, and a stronger immune system? Would you like to sleep better, improve your cognitive and athletic performance, boost your mood, lose weight, and alleviate your anxiety? What if I told you that you can achieve all these things and so much more by unlocking the power of your own mind? And that you can do it in only a few days?

As humanity has evolved and developed technology that has made us more and more comfortable, we have lost our innate ability not only to survive but to thrive in extreme environments. In the absence of environmental stress, the things we have built to make our lives easier have actually made us weaker. But what if we could reawaken the dormant physiological processes that made our ancestors so strong?

My method, which I have developed and refined over the course of nearly forty years, is based on three simple, natural pillars: cold exposure, conscious breathing, and the power of the mind. I have employed this method to accomplish feats believed by many to be impossible, setting more than two dozen Guinness World Records and confounding medical professionals in the process. That includes running a half marathon above the Arctic Circle while barefoot, wearing only shorts, and a full marathon through Africa's Namib Desert, without drinking any water. It includes swimming underneath a thick layer of ice for more than two hundred feet and standing packed in ice for hours at a time without my core body temperature dropping. I've summited some of the world's highest mountains dressed only in shorts. It's true.

Doing these things has earned me the nickname the Iceman, but I am no superhero. I am no genetic freak. I'm not a guru, and I did not invent these techniques either. Cold exposure and conscious breathing have been practiced for thousands of years. I do not mention my accomplishments to boast, but as a reminder that there is so much more we are capable of. I want to ignite your awe of your body, your mind, and your beautiful humanity. I invite you to witness your own being blossoming, to push past your conditioning. This method is accessible to all. Anything I can do, you can do just as well. I know this because I have spent the past fifteen years turning skeptics into believers. I have taught the method all over the world and seen the remarkable results firsthand. People who have embraced my method have been able to reverse diabetes; relieve the debilitating symptoms of Parkinson's disease, rheumatoid arthritis, and multiple sclerosis; and address a host of other autoimmune illnesses, from lupus to Lyme disease.[1]

The secret to a lifetime of health and happiness is within your grasp. You can safely practice the Wim Hof Method by yourself, at your own pace, and within the comfort of your own home. No pills, injections, vitamins, supplements, equipment, or specialty diets of any kind—all you need is yourself and a desire to unlock your body's hidden potential. This book is your guide.

Are you ready? In the pages that follow, I will share the story of my journey, from the small Dutch village in which I was born to the world stage I now occupy. I will explain the ins and outs of my method, the philosophy that underpins it, and the science that supports it. And I will present examples of practitioners who have used the method to radically transform their lives. In doing so, my hope is to inspire you to retake control of your body and life by unleashing the immense power of your mind. It's all there for you, and there's no time to waste.

Let's go.

1

THE MISSIONARY

The breath is a door. Without the breath, what is there? It's where you and I and everyone else began. It's where all life begins.

I am a twin, but at the time of my birth in 1959 in the Netherlands, there were no echo devices to detect that there was a second baby in the womb. So, I was still there when my mother was taken back to her bed to recover after delivering my brother, Andre. She felt a strangeness inside of her. There was something there still, but she did not know what it was. And, of course, within the turbulence of childbirth, women will experience many disorienting sensations.

But what happened? She felt strange after giving birth to Andre. And as she had already delivered four children previously, she knew she was not mistaken. She had never felt this way after any of her other deliveries. So, there she was in the recovery room, and she said, "There is something else there, doctor." The doctor, however, was dismissive. "That's what happens after the birth," he said. "It's just some additional contractions, that's all." The doctor went away, and my mother was again left alone in the room to recover. But the feeling inside of her only intensified, and at a certain moment, she knew that there was another baby. She began to yell for the nurses, and *finally*, after several visits from nurses attempting to reassure her that the doctor was right—that it was contractions and she shouldn't worry, it will all fade away—they found out that, yes, there was indeed another one. But not only that, this other baby was bound to die if they didn't intervene at that exact moment.

They wheeled the bed back to the operating room to get me out because they determined that I was in too deep to be delivered naturally. And that put my mother into an altered state of consciousness, in which she fixated on the dreadful thought that her child might die. Just before arriving to the operating room, she yelled, "Oh, God, let this child live! I will make him a missionary!" She feared that they were going to cut into her, that she would lose the birth. In that moment, the power of fear roused the strength of her unwavering belief. My mother was very strong, pious, and intelligent, a devout Catholic. Before beginning our family at age twenty-eight, she had been working in an office and was very independent. Yet in those days, women could not work anymore after having children. They had to stay home, and the man had to provide the work. She already had three children at home when we were born and proceeded to have another four after that—each one, she felt, a gift from God. She took to having children as if it were her Catholic duty and carried that same practical, down-to-earth, headstrong attitude into raising her children. She wasn't educated much formally. Her father and mother had been farmers, and she and her siblings struggled with the absence of their mother, who became schizophrenic and was institutionalized. Their father raised the kids all by himself, which at that time was quite rare.

Now my mother, with her very strong belief in God, was attempting through her faith to invoke me into the world. And in the cold of the hallway, I was born through a force unknown to her or anybody because of the circumstances. Possibly many more children were and will be born like that, in very extreme conditions—perhaps even more extreme. But what is karma? What is destiny? I don't know. And at that moment I was just a little bit of nothing. I was purple because I almost suffocated. I was cold. But I had been invoked by my mother so strongly, like a tattoo on my soul, without having any point of reference for what was going on. I was just a piece of nothing. Helpless. But then I began to breathe.

That's the way I started my life. I barely survived. And, of course, I can't really remember what happened, but my mother told the story many times. Perhaps as a result of my unusual beginning, I've always had a yearning for something else, for something more, something deeper, mystical — something strange. I remember at the age of four, I had a moment of epiphany that made me stop completely. I just saw light. Light! *What is this?* It overwhelmed me. I wasn't thinking, I was just in the light. But what was it? I didn't know then, and I still don't know. But the memory is indelible.

Andre and I shared a tiny room and the same bed for sixteen years. We shared a love of the unusual and would save our money and spend it on exotic plants. But even with our similarities, I always felt different. I was fascinated by pictures we had on the walls of the temples of Tibet. By the age of twelve, I was already into yoga, Hinduism, Buddhism — what one might call esoteric disciplines — as well as psychology. But I was not the best student in my family. My mother was loving and caring, but very strict, very eager for us to be cognitively sharp. We had no money, as my father had health issues that kept him from working regularly. Conventional intelligence was the emotional currency of the time. My older brothers strived to become the best in school, but I had no chance of that. Along with Andre, we were nicknamed the PeePee's, and we were inseparable, and at times it felt that we were one. But I always felt something like the black sheep of sorts, a little more strange, excitable, just different.

When I was seven years old, I remember playing in a snowy pasture with my friends, constructing a sort of igloo. You know, whatever you imagine an igloo might look like when you're seven. After a while, all my friends went home, but I stayed behind. And this rosy feeling came over me and made me just sit down in the snow. It got late, and my parents and brothers began looking for me because I wasn't home. It wasn't unusual for me to play outside in the forest near our home in Sittard, making cabins and playing Tarzan and all that like kids do, but now I was in the snow.[1] I loved the snow then as I do now. But I had been out there so long that they became worried. When they found me, I had already been sleeping for quite some time, and I resisted when they woke me. I later learned that I was experiencing the onset of what's referred to as "the white death" where you can doze off, become hypothermic, fall into a coma, and then the rest is done. I mean, it's truly irreversible if no external heat source is applied.[2] So they picked me up out of the snow and took me home, and it was actually quite terrible getting back because I was hypothermic. But I recovered.

At the age of eleven, the same thing happened. I went to school, and on my way home, I decided that I wanted to sit down. The weather was cold and freezing, and I just sat down on a neighbor's porch and slept. I don't know what happened exactly, but apparently an ambulance arrived after someone telephoned to say they saw a young kid sleeping in freezing temperatures outside. I woke up in the hospital, and they kept me there for observation for a week. Again, I recovered, but I was aware that I could have died in either of those moments if someone hadn't woken me and taken me into a warm area. The strange thing about hypothermia is that you don't want to wake up; you just want to go to sleep. Why that is, I don't know exactly, but those were my first encounters with the cold. And despite the very real danger they both posed, they were actually quite nice. I felt rosy. You go to sleep, and that's it. Thank you very much, goodbye life. It's okay. No worries. No fears. No nothing. Just a nice, rosy feeling.

Another time when I was young, maybe six years old, my friends and I were playing near the forest. One of them threw a bottle of dirty water from the local brook on me, which was actually sewer water full of bacteria, and I became very sick. The fellow who had poured the bottle over me harbored no malicious intent, I don't believe. He was just being mischievous, but at the same time imposing his will over me by saying, in effect, "I'm eight years old and much bigger than you, and look what I can do to you." I can still remember that feeling of powerlessness. I couldn't do anything because he was just a much bigger and older guy than me, so I had little choice but to take his abuse and go home. And when I did, I spent the next two nights vomiting green before my parents finally took me to the hospital. As it turned out, I had contracted Weil syndrome (or leptospirosis), which is a rare, very infectious disease.[3] The infection was so serious that I remained hospitalized for three weeks, but, of course, I recovered well. Those moments mark my earliest encounters with the snow and bacterial infection, both of which would play big roles later in my life. In that, I suppose these episodes were harbingers of what was to come.

From a young age I have been drawn to storytelling. Whenever people began to tell stories, *real* stories, of something out there, something strange, something deep, I was completely intrigued by and focused on their words. They could swallow me in the vortex of their telling. Otherwise, I was a very playful kid. I enjoyed playing Tarzan, and I loved spending time outdoors in the forest. We played by making cabins in the trees and hanging and going from tree to tree with "vines" that we made out of old bicycle tires. We'd tie them to each other, hang them over the branches, and then swing from one tree to another making Tarzan's jungle call as loudly as we could because we were the apes. We were playing the apes, and we loved it. We *were* Tarzan.

Because we really loved being outdoors, my twin brother and I would venture, whenever we had time, into nature, into the forest. We'd be gone all day making cabins, climbing trees, digging underground, and baking potatoes in the little fire we'd build. To this day I believe those potatoes were the best food I've ever eaten. With just a little bit of salt, they were so delicious, so exquisite. They represented our freedom, and no restaurant could ever match their flavor because we ate them in connection with nature. Being outdoors heightened all of our senses. I think nowadays many children miss out on that. They're so involved with their computers and games and virtual realities that they lose sight of the true reality: nature, which stimulates, develops, and sharpens their senses. This disconnection from nature contributes, I think, to depression and other problems, which is unfortunate.

While it's true that by the age of twelve I was exploring psychology, Hinduism, Buddhism, and yoga, it's also true that I served, like so many of my peers growing up, as an altar boy. This, of course, was because of my mother, who was a devout Catholic. She was pious and therefore required her children to attend church with her every Sunday. But while I tried in earnest out of respect for my dear mother, I just couldn't feel a connection to church and instead found the experience quite boring. Because of this boredom, I always had an adverse feeling toward attending church services, but my mother insisted that it was our moral obligation to do so. And there was no escaping from a mother like that. Not my mother. She held her grip on us really tightly, and my siblings and I were therefore forced to endure countless Sundays at church in which, in my juvenile perspective, nothing much was going on. I was a boy built for Saturdays. On Saturdays I could go into the woods, get myself dirty, do my Tarzan shout at the top of my lungs. On Saturdays I could run through the forest, build something out of nothing, invent a thousand games. I could lose myself in the freedom of play. A forest is like a wonderland for a child with a creative imagination. It is nothing like church.

At thirteen I decided to embrace vegetarianism, which was a radical thing for a young person—or anyone—to do in the culture in which I lived, where everybody ate meat and considered it a perfectly normal thing to do. But I had recently made the acquaintance of an older gentleman who was, in his way, protesting against that culture. It was almost Christmastime, and he said, "If God has a consciousness, and this is the time for peace on Earth, how can it also be the time of the greatest mass slaughtering?" How can that be? So I began to think about the animals we consume and the way they are treated by the meat industry, and I came to see the cruelty of it. Live animals were being delivered by trucks and being killed. There was nothing natural about it, no hunter-gatherer human element. It was just slaughtering and cruelty. For what?

The more I thought about it, the more determined I became to decrease the amount of meat I consumed each day. I resolved to be mindful and to see it through, and a couple of months later, I was no longer a meat-eater. With the culture being what it was at the time, this instantly branded me as different—although my family took it in stride as just another strange thing about me. Suddenly I was a different duck in the pond. It seemed as if everybody were looking and pointing at me, saying, "You're different, you're different." And I was.

I nurtured my independence, building my own little world. By becoming a vegetarian, exploring esoteric disciplines, and wearing my hair long like a hippie, I was beginning to segregate from the normal culture. I suffered from efforts to suppress my nature, as many people do. Once I accepted that I was different, and made my peace with it, I began to segregate even further, specifically with respect to my consciousness and the way I perceived the world around me. I was a sensitive boy. I learned to develop my own way.

I was never a very good student. When it came to history, language, mathematics, science, and all, my grades were just average. Not bad, mind you, but not exceptional either, and I was convinced that I couldn't gain entry to the higher schooling that my high-achieving brothers did. For large families of that time, doing well in school was a matter of survival. Others impressed upon me how those who attend the best schools go on to the best universities, which leads to great careers and all the attention that comes with that kind of success, so I enrolled in a weekend course in which I could prove myself in spite of my limitations as a student. By talking and participating actively in discussions, I managed to pass the course in six weeks and was admitted into the higher schooling. But it didn't take long for me to see that this kind of schooling wasn't for me, and I ended up staying for only three quarters of a year before dropping out.

Yes, I'm a dropout, and I'm not at all ashamed. I'm a dropout who now teaches professors and doctors all over the world. The work I'm doing is breaking ground and rewriting the scientific literature at least partially *because* I am a dropout. Being out of the loop and unaware of what was going on in academic circles caused me to just follow the natural flow of things and try to survive in society on the strength of my intuition and instincts. Society on the whole is very much fixated on the achievement of tangible results and becoming something definable to others. A lawyer, a banker, whatever. But that wasn't my path. My instincts and intuition were leading me in a different direction, and that's because of my mother. She had not only invocated but imprinted this in the very depths of my DNA, of my soul and spirit. From birth, I was bound to follow a different mission. That doesn't make me special or unique, but I do believe that life is special, and we should treat it that way.

2 THE BIRTH OF THE ICEMAN

Sittard, my hometown in the southernmost section of the Netherlands, is located just over a half mile from Germany and seven and a half miles from Belgium, in the narrowest part of the country. So as a young man, I was influenced by both German and Belgian culture, by both their French- and German-speaking populations, and then, of course by our own Dutch language and culture. From the ages of twelve to seventeen, I delivered newspapers, both *Algemeen Dagblad* and *De Telegraaf*, in the early morning hours. That is a very different dimension of the day, when nobody is around and you are there in sync with your bicycle and the elements of nature.

I've always been a simple guy, and I'll remain a simple guy. I love my old bicycle much more than all the fancy, new, glittering, iridescent bikes on the market today, with all their toys and devices. I rode an old bike to Spain three times and once almost to Africa. I don't know what it was about those old bikes, really, but they got to me.

The area where I was delivering the newspapers was a little bit hilly, which could make carrying a heavy load a challenge. I'd ride up a hill with a basketful of newspapers, and it would be so heavy (the thick Saturday edition, especially) that I'd stop halfway up the hill, deliver the

The historic market square of Sittard, my hometown in the Netherlands

newspapers, and then go on. It made me stronger. Eventually I beat the hills. And in a contest that took place at a festival in Sittard, I clocked a kilometer on a stationary bike in one minute, two seconds. I didn't think much of it until a professional cyclist finished at one minute, four, and then another at one minute, six. I won the contest. All those mornings delivering newspapers on those hills no matter the weather made me stronger, and not just physically. It taught me discipline.

Every day for five years, I woke up at 3:30 a.m. I'd roll out of my bed directly into the push-up position, do fifty push-ups, and then I'd be awake. My father would serve me and my brothers each a big cup of coffee, and we'd be out the door by 4:00 a.m. to our paper routes. It was a precise routine. Then I'd go out into the night with these packs full of newspapers, up and down the hills of Sittard. I'd hear all kinds of birds and see rabbits on the street, and it was just all so magical and contemplative. I saw and felt things that, because I was alone, didn't require words. It was just me and my bicycle and the newspapers alone in the hills. Every day for five years.

That experience absolutely formed the fundamental layer of my disciplinary morals. I was strong as a special-forces soldier in the military. So I recommend that any kid, if he or she wants to be strong, deliver newspapers in a hilly area. You get to know who you are because there's nobody else around to talk to. You begin to contemplate; you see the world in peace without the rumor of anything or anybody. You are alone, and you have to fulfill a task regardless of the weather conditions. You find yourself in the depth of yourself. That's strength.

With that newfound strength and all of its attendant confidence, I took off on a bicycle, at the age of seventeen, with my twin brother, to Spain. Thousands of miles on a bike. I still had the old newspaper bags, so I just filled them with some essential items. It was a beautiful experience. October in the Netherlands is when fall really sets in and when cold weather begins to mix with the rain, which is very cold. Cycling with rainwater on our skin greatly intensified our bodies' induction to the cold, as water does, so we really did get cold. But we pressed on anyway, through the Ardennes mountains in Belgium. I remember snow and very cold temperatures. At one point, we had to stop because we needed to eat, but the only food we had brought with us was oats, dry oats, which tasted to me like hazelnuts. Amazing.

If you immerse yourself in nature, in the elements, so much that your body is working in its depth and all the senses of your being are truly activated, and you eat only when your body requires it as opposed to at fixed meal times, you will find that your appetite shifts in such a profound way that even dry oats become like a feast. We have mostly lost this connection today, this deep sense, and thus, many of us aren't able to incorporate its values into our everyday life. But back then, out on the cold roads on our bicycles, we felt it deeply, and we have carried that feeling with us in our hearts ever since.

Andre and I cycled down through the Ardennes and slowly but surely neared the Mediterranean area of the south of France, the Côte d'Azur. And throughout our ride, we saw the change not only of the weather, which became better and better, but also of the vegetation, the architecture, and the behavior of people. As temperatures get warmer, people come outside more, talk more to each other, and paint their houses more colorfully. October in the south of France is a wonderful time, and from there, we followed the sunshine to Spain, where it was harvest time for melons, oranges, and figs. We had a marvelous time picking all of these fruits, looking around, and, you know, traveling by bicycle is just different. It's not like traveling by car. Sitting in a car is like watching television; you just sit and watch what is happening outside your window. But when you travel by bicycle, you charge up your feelings, you look around, and everything is amplified because you forge a direct connection with it all. More than forty years later, I can still taste those fruits, smell the sweetness of that air. I can feel it still, now in my sixties.

One of my goals is to make these feelings, these deeper feelings of being in connection with nature, understood by all. You are Tarzan. You are Jane. You are a king. You are a queen. The corona is not only a symbol to place upon the head of a man called "king," but an aura that surrounds you when you radiate, when your brain is fully alive. You radiate an electromagnetic field, and that's the corona. That energy is what makes you a king or a queen. It's a natural coronation. So comport yourself as a king or a queen and stand proudly in your corona because that's who you are inside.

I didn't know it, but I was looking for exactly that back then. That connection. I was looking for something within me that I couldn't quite articulate but, with time and experience, I began to know. My mother's invocation really was the redline of my history. A mother's power is good and full of love because it comes from nature. Better listen to it. She knows. She is there. And that's the way it should be. I took my mother's love, her invocation, and began, at seventeen, to really dig consciously into these deeper layers of myself, gaining a keen awareness that there was more to the world and to myself than met the eye. There was much unseen, and I yearned desperately to see it.

I knew a bit of French, and I used it to communicate with the people we encountered on our journey. And while my vocabulary was limited, I was still able to relate to these people because I was giving them something that went beyond language and that came instead from within me, from my heart. It was a feeling, a deep feeling that I now understand more fully, but at the time I was just feeling it. Meeting people who were more exuberant and open liberated my mind.

It enabled me to reconcile with the parts of myself that others deemed weird or different. And the farther south we traveled, the farther away from the Netherlands, from our conditioned cultural beliefs and experiences, the closer I felt to myself. It brought some epiphanies. I was able to shake off the sense of prejudice I usually felt. It's amazing what can happen within your core if you get there, if you meet the light within yourself. You just know it. I'm convinced that everybody who goes consciously into that light is searching and looking for the same thing: purpose.

Near the border of France and Spain, in the Pyrenees, Andre and I met a man named Wolfgang. Wolfgang was German and a bit older than we were. Half the year he would work in Germany as a nurse, and for the other half of the year, he would hop on his bike and cycle to Africa. He had already completed two of those rides by the time we met, and I remember he told a story about traveling through the Sudanese desert — the Sahara — and walking beside his bike because he could not ride it in the sand. He was walking along the path, and

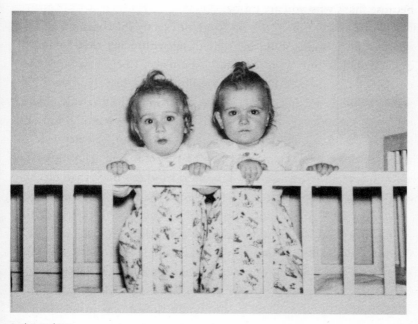

Andre and me

at a certain moment, out of nowhere, there was a lion! The lion saw him and probably also the reflection of the sun on his bike or something, and it ran away. But for Wolfgang, as you might imagine, that was a startling moment. But it didn't stop him from taking that same route a second time.

The other thing I remember about Wolfgang is that he listened intently to everything I had to say. Here I was a boy of seventeen, green, just coming into an understanding of myself, while he was a man of considerable experience for someone just a few years older than me. He treated me and my ideas with respect, never dismissiveness. He could sense that I was searching for something within the depth of myself without fully knowing what it was and that he could learn from me. But as I spoke to him, I became acutely conscious of the fact that I was telling things to an older person, someone experienced in world traveling. A man who had encountered a solitary lion in the wild and lived to tell the tale. I mean, what kind of fear could a man like that possibly have? A man with the courage to work half a year as a nurse and then travel for half a year alone on a bicycle straight through Africa? There was no fear. He just knew. And I didn't, at least not yet. I was just there. But it was in that moment that I began to become aware that I could also know and, perhaps more importantly, believe that I could.

This was a monumental epiphany for me. Becoming aware that such knowing was possible freed me from my own fear and sent me in the direction of that knowledge. Natural wisdom, coming from the core, inside, is something that we all possess innately, I realized, but sometimes we are too conditioned within to recognize it, or to believe it. Too often we mistake this knowledge for dreams or, worse, folly. But there I was on my bicycle in the south of France and into Spain now, past the Pyrenees, meeting and talking with Wolfgang about philosophy and other far-out topics, and having a great time of it. Andre would listen in sometimes, but most of the time, he stayed about a quarter mile in front of us. Andre is much more down-to-earth than me, more practical, you could say. He let us talk on, we were so engrossed in our conversation, and he didn't want to intrude on that. There was such a depth to our dialogue that I experienced a cascade of epiphanies, first coming into an understanding of true contemplation. It was through this contemplation that I was able to go where I had never gone before, become aware, and bring all these energies within me into my consciousness. I realized that we all have this sacred spot within us, and it became my aim to access it. Once you can do that, you become aware of your own light, your own being, your own purpose. It's all there for you if you know where to look.

I remember one day waking up in a melon field and feeling quite different. I didn't know what it was. I looked once again within myself, and there it was. This energy that connects the brain with the deeper parts of the mind and forges a deeper understanding; that's what came into my consciousness that morning. There was no dualism. The mind and nature are one. That's it. It was disorienting at first waking up and feeling differently than always. I didn't know what it was, but it was me all the same. A new me who had been there all along. Transcendent. And for the three weeks that followed, I remained in that transcendent state of being. But then we returned to the Netherlands and came back into the turmoil of things, into the conditioning, into everything and everybody and that whole trip.

I lived in those times, at the age of seventeen, in a squatter's home. At that time in the Netherlands, squatting was somewhat of an accepted practice.[1] Some people possess more property than they know what to do with, and for that, you get squatters. Squatters are people who just go in and say, "You're speculating on this property to profit from the real estate market and, meanwhile, there's nobody inside. That's not right! It's your property, but it's living space, and we have no place to live. So we'll take it for now and pay the gas and the electricity, and that's it." That was my feeling. I was a squatter, a protester. I believed that what was right was right and that we had an obligation to make what was wrong right or, at very least, stand up in opposition. And I lived there in that home as a squatter for eight years. That time represented a period of true freedom for me because there were absolutely no rules. I was already an outcast from society, living outside of the system, and squatting only served to reinforce and widen my segregation from society. It forced me further and further inward, and I was able to think freely and to make a lot of music.

Perhaps today, in the Netherlands and in other countries, like the United States, squatting is a more dangerous proposition, but that was an idyllic time in my life. It was a place of pure freedom. About a hundred people lived together in peaceful coexistence and creative abundance. With the pressure of fitting into society and making a living more or less removed, people in that space were able to just let go and respond to their creative urges. So we had a lot of art over there, a lot of music. Festivals. Talking. And the energy was free. I made a lot of music in those years, debated a lot, and I have to say, my sense of free thinking was developed there.

While I concede that squatting isn't for everyone, especially today, I do believe that everyone should have a time, a space in his or her life, in which he or she is able to live free like that, if only as a sabbatical. You retreat from society because you want to free your own mind, but first you have to learn to let it go. What good is it to detach from all the rules, morals, and ethics of a repressive system if you're not able to express yourself? That's just inviting a different kind of stress. So there I was, for eight years, expressing myself. I was living freely in a place where creative expression was valued as it should be. But at the same time, I became very disciplined. Discipline served as a way to liberate myself. And then, one quiet Sunday morning in the wintertime, I was in Beatrixpark pondering it all, and I saw this thin layer of ice on the water.

I felt an attraction to it that I couldn't quite explain, but I looked around, and there was nobody else in sight. I could undress myself and just go naked into the cold water, which is exactly what I did. I remember very clearly that I wasn't bothered by the cold at all, I was just curious. That curiosity was much stronger than the temperature of the water. Can you imagine that? But while now I know why that was, back then I simply experienced it.[2] And that cold water had an unexpected effect on my body, which is that I felt great. I was playing with a thin layer of ice all around me, feeling astonished that I had the ability to just play in it. I was looking at the ice—not understanding yet, just looking—and thinking to myself, *Wow, I can play!*

I'm in the water! And it's fine! Everybody always said it was crazy to go into the cold water. You could die, they said. It's no good! It's an adverse element of nature, and we have to protect ourselves from it! That's what we had been conditioned to believe, but all of that vanished in this moment. I felt great. I wasn't in the water for too long, maybe a minute, a minute and a half, but long enough to feel the connection, borne to my consciousness, within. Beyond language or intellectual framing.

Now we can understand that the strength of my curiosity being greater than the cold of the water was a demonstration of the human mind's immense power. But sadly, mankind as a whole has lost its connection to this power because we rarely, if ever, venture out into the elements anymore. We stay snugged-up in our cozy, heated homes, safe from the environmental stressors that enable this power to rise within us. Thus, our minds are not able to transcend the impact of extreme forces on our bodies or to accept the truth of mind over matter. I know it's the truth and have dedicated most of my life to demonstrating it. For decades, I faced the scorn and incredulity of imaginationless naysayers. But it all began in earnest right there. It was the origin point of my entire quest. I felt terrific coming out of the water — just astonished, not really thinking — just feeling the rush of endorphins and going home feeling great.

I returned to the water a few days later and did the same thing with the same results. Of course, whenever you feel as good about something as I did about this, you're bound to come back often. So that's what I did, time and again. I began to notice that I would involuntarily gasp each time I immersed myself, and I found this intriguing. And when, at a certain moment, I did twenty-five deep breaths, it made my body tingle like crazy, like electricity. I'm not entirely sure why I decided to breathe in that way in the moment, but it was likely just my gut feeling, an impulse that I acted upon and then followed my own guide therein. Going into the water makes you breathe deeper and more consciously. The carbon dioxide goes out, and the muscles begin to contract. It's basic physiology. But it's also that electricity, the autonomic nervous system, at work. It was an amazing feeling, and over time, a routine gradually took shape. It was organic and progressive,

and this physical experience of the cold and following my gut led me to a true personal discovery of my own consciousness, my own mind-body connection. I was only seventeen, and I felt alive and excited.

With practice, I'd be so fully charged by my breathing practice that the trigger to breathe wasn't really there. I got to where I could go for over five minutes without taking a breath. At the same time, I was experimenting with swimming in the icy water. I did this day in, day out, all winter long, for twenty-five years in a row. Over that time, I learned how to consciously control my body. It didn't happen overnight, but I remember sitting outside one freezing night wearing nothing but shorts and feeling great about it. I felt great because I knew that I was on to something. And I was. The Iceman had been born.

3

A COLD SHOWER A DAY KEEPS THE DOCTOR AWAY

There is so much more to life than meets the eye if you choose to seek it. The seeker becomes the finder, the finder of so much more than we thought was possible. Most of us are raised to follow a familiar, predictable path: you go to school, choose a career, and then, if you are lucky, you earn a sabbatical, maybe a raise. This experience defines us, but it is not us. There is much, much, much more to our existence than that, to who we are in our depth. Our soul. And in accessing that soul, we find out that our minds and bodies are capable of so much more. We are beings of light who, by birthright, own our own minds and souls. This is the time to wake up to the true power we each possess within us. By consciously connecting with the reptilian brain, previously believed to be inaccessible, we have arrived at a new frontier, that of the brain-over-body consciousness. That consciousness allows you to truly trust your judgment based on intuition and instinct. I arrived at these insights by going into the cold water, by reconditioning my mind and body to reject the primordial, prehistoric feeling that the cold is our enemy and that we have to make fire and sit in the cave to combat it. We have nothing to combat but our own conditioning and fear.

My American friend Chris Ryan wrote a book entitled *Civilized to Death* on these deeper feelings, about how we have become so civilized, so ensconced in our comfort zones, that it has gotten the better of us. He argues that we don't live in nature anymore, but in opposition to it. And what, in the end, are we really opposing? The cold and its adverse power are not our enemy! The cold knows how to trigger our vascular system, which, if laid out end-to-end, would stretch nearly two and a half times the length of the world.[1] Cardiovascular-related diseases are the number-one killer in our society today, but it doesn't have to be that way.[2] There are approximately sixty-two thousand miles of veins, arteries, and capillaries in each and every one of us.[3] The vascular system is constructed, after millions of years of evolution, with millions of little muscles that contract and open the veins and the vascular channels in reaction to the weather. Regardless of if it is warm or hot, our core body temperature has to remain 98.6 degrees Fahrenheit. If your core temperature dips only 2 or 3 degrees below that, you go into hypothermia, a hypothermic state. If it dips 3 degrees or more than that, it's irreversible; your core body temperature spirals down, and your body is no longer able to heat up. So, we have this vascular system that opens and closes to protect ourselves from the cold and heat, to remain within the range of normal body temperatures. It's a very delicate system.

But what did we do? We got into clothes. And we love these clothes so much, these dresses and suits and nice ties. They're wonderful! We've got Gucci, Versace, Vanderbilt, all these fashions that everybody loves. But clothes actually de-stimulate our vascular system, the intricate system that delivers blood throughout our bodies. And when the elements are working on our vascular system, it opens and closes, it expands and contracts, and in doing so, the muscular tone of the vascular system is exercised. But wearing clothes, being dressed up all the time, is de-stimulating. These little muscles do not work. And do you know who's paying for that? Our heart is. When these little vascular muscles are not tuned up, not working at an optimized condition, our heart is forced to pump much more, deeper and stronger, to get the blood flow through. This puts undue stress on our heart on a chronic basis. That's one of the primary reasons, together with diet and exercise, why cardiovascular-related diseases are the number-one killer in our society.

How do we tackle this killer? It's very simple. A cold shower a day keeps the doctor away. The medical system is increasingly driven more by pharmaceutical solutions than by healing, and few would recommend this method, but it's right there. It's simple, and it works, and it doesn't cost a thing. Our vascular system needs to be stimulated to achieve the desired muscular tone. It doesn't need training, only awakening. Then, once it's awakened and optimized, let's say in ten days, a whole sequence of magic begins to occur within the body.

Anybody who has ever stepped into an unheated swimming pool or endured an "Ice Bucket Challenge" knows that the immediate impact of cold water on our bodies can be uncomfortable, if not downright painful. It is therefore understandable why some might be reluctant to willingly submit to that discomfort. It's unpleasant. But just as your body adjusts, in time, to the water in the swimming pool, so does it adjust, with repeated exposure, to the water in the cold shower. Initially, the cold water will precipitate a cold shock response, or a gasp reflex, which is a completely natural reaction. This may lead to some hyperventilation, yet this involuntary physiological response subsides over time as the body relaxes and begins to adjust to its new environment. The more often you take cold showers and the more accustomed you get to that initial shock, the more you begin to crave the sensation.

I began intuitively, when I was seventeen years old, to venture into the cold water. I understand now that this intuition stemmed from the trauma of my birth, but that's my personal story. It doesn't matter how you get to it so long as you do, and if you get there from my suggestion, then all the better. I have dedicated my life to this because I have experienced the benefits firsthand. Back then I had a feeling, and I could not find an explanation for it in the books I was reading. Couldn't find it. So I went into nature, and I found answers that weren't in books. And because nature belongs to all of us, I feel compelled to share what I have learned. It's not mine, it's ours. I just simplified it. We are able, as a society, to confront cardiovascular-related diseases if we can learn, collectively, how to achieve vascular fitness.

When you take a cold shower, all of those little muscles in your vascular system—millions of them—are activated and exercised. Within ten days of taking these showers, you will notice that your heart rate has decreased significantly, as much as fifteen to thirty beats per minute, and that it remains that way twenty-four hours a day. That translates to a lot less stress. It's important to understand that your heart rate increases whenever your body experiences stress. That sends a primordial signal to the body to activate adrenaline and cortisol, which sets off a series of biochemical processes that exhaust your adrenal axis, your energy, because you're in poor vascular condition. Your heart needs to pump more, work harder.

At the same time, while your energy is depleted, you've got your boss telling you to do this or that, your spouse is making their own demands, and your children are doing what children do, all of which increase your stress levels. Traffic on the roadways or mass-transit delays don't help either. It all adds up, and the result is that your heart has to pump even more without any way to cool down, to have a rest, because your vascular system is compromised.

Now, if you go and exercise your vascular system—I call it "vascular fitness" nowadays—you can effectively counteract this stress. Once you have trained yourself with exposure to cold, you can do "snowga," which is, like it sounds, yoga in the snow. You can go and do exercises outdoors in the cold while bare-chested and barefoot, just in shorts. Within fifteen minutes, you won't feel the cold, which is an indication that your vascular system has adapted. That's innate. It was always there, but by constantly seeking comfort, we have become strangers to our natural, optimized vascular condition. This is unfortunate because it's our vascular system that delivers blood to the cells and with it, all the nutrients, oxygen, and vitamins our bodies need to thrive. And if your vascular system is exercised and adapted, your heart rate will decrease in turn. It's the antidote to stress, and it all starts with cold showers.

Cold showers are the gateway to flow and energy and peace. I'm not exaggerating. It's the entry point from which you will learn the power of the mind over the body. If you do just ten days of cold showers after warm showers, meaning that you end your regular, warm showers with a minute or so of cold water, then you will be able to command your vascular system to close up when you go into the cold. It's amazing what your body can do at will, and all it takes is ten days of these showers to regain your optimal vascular tone and achieve this control. As your vascular system awakens and its muscles begin to tone up, it forges a connection with your brain, with your will.

WHM PROTOCOL:
COLD EXPOSURE FOR BEGINNERS

Going into the ice water can be quite shocking, so you'd better learn to prepare your body if you want to try it. But how do you do that? We wear clothes all the time, which de-stimulates our bodies, leaving our vascular systems in poor condition. So what can we do to reduce the impact of the shock and instead allow the ice water to optimize our cardiovascular system? Most of us who live in the West take showers every day, and most of those are warm or hot showers, because we don't like the cold. But if you end your warm or hot shower with just thirty seconds of cold water—just thirty seconds—you will begin to see results.

Anybody is able to endure thirty seconds of cold water, especially after spending several minutes under the warm or hot water, collecting heat. The warm water opens up your veins, aiding your blood flow. So while the cold water might cause you some discomfort at first, thirty seconds is no great hardship.

What happens inside your body when you shift the temperature from warm to cold is that all the little muscles in your vascular system begin to awaken. They close up and then open, close up and open, and this repetitive process establishes the vascular muscle tone that, with repeated exposure, develops into its optimal condition. Start slowly at the beginning, with just fifteen seconds at the end of your shower every day. In a week, you will feel able to endure thirty seconds, or more. This is because the tone of your vascular muscles is improving, developing. Your core body temperature remains just fine. And the result is that you experience better blood flow throughout the day, which gives you a lot more energy. Once you are able to go longer than thirty seconds, you begin to develop an ability to consciously resist the shock of the cold water. You suppress the shiver response, the gasp. Suddenly, the water's not cold anymore. Instead, it's a force, and you, standing there, are a counterforce. You're in control. You're awakening to the physiological power and the neural activity of your own body. Amazing.

WEEK 1 Thirty seconds of cold water at the end of a warm shower
WEEK 2 One minute of cold water at the end of a warm shower
WEEK 3 A minute and a half of cold water at the end of a warm shower
WEEK 4 Two minutes of cold water at the end of a warm shower

Do this gradually and work your way up, at least five days a week. Follow the feeling. Don't force anything. It's also fine to start with fifteen seconds and build up more slowly, as we do in our 20-Day Cold Shower Challenge.

Some benefits of cold exposure begin at 60° Fahrenheit, so most tap water is cold enough to make a difference. As your vascular muscle tone develops, it will absorb more and more of the shock until it's hardly a shock at all. Your vascular system constricts on demand to protect your vital parts. And what you will see is that your heart rate goes down during the day, reducing your stress level. You feel more energized. The improved blood flow delivers better nutrition to your cells. You find that you don't get sick anymore because your body is no longer vulnerable. Instead, you feel strong.

By the end of the fourth week, your vascular tone will be optimized to the point that it will be mind over matter. You turn the knob to cold and will your body not to react in shock. This is only the beginning of the power of the mind opening up to you. If you are able to command the vascular system, which is everywhere within your body, you are able to go, at will, to any part and control it consciously. You're the boss. And it all starts with thirty seconds of cold water.

When prehistoric humans ventured forth out of their caves and into the wild, they had to be strong. They needed the vascular system to close up to protect the core body temperature, which was necessary not only to function, but to survive. Otherwise they would risk hypothermia and death. So a prehistoric man knew, when he went out to hunt, that his body would respond accordingly. And automatically.

By closing up, his extremities and the rest of his body would be able to brave the elements without endangering his core body temperature, which would remain the same, protecting the function of its vital organs: the liver, heart, lungs, and brain. The rest of the body can get quite cold, but if the vascular tone is not right, the body doesn't respond. Then, when we get out into the cold, the vascular system doesn't close well, and we get sick.

And that's the thing. Worrying parents have forever implored their children to bundle up with heavy coats, hats, and scarves to avoid catching cold. But the truth is that it's having a weaker vascular system that has, in turn, made us and our children weak and susceptible to illness. If we take cold showers though, we can regain the lost, optimized condition of our vascular tone and in turn become strong. We will become able to act naturally within heat and cold and withstand all the elements of nature without significantly impacting our core body temperature. And it's amazing what kinds of health benefits stem from there. Not only is it good for our vascular system, which again is the transportation system for all of the vitamins, oxygen, and nutrients our cells need, it also relieves the cells of biological stress. With that comes peace. Deep peace.

When we get our vascular muscles into the proper tone, our blood flow—our life-force—is able to communicate so much to our brain about peace and about life because without blood, we are like nothing. And it's all there in the cold. By exercising and toning those muscles, we can go into the cold with the appropriate attitude. We can see the cold not as an adversarial, malignant, or negative power, but instead as a mirror that reflects whether or not our body is responding the right way, the way nature intended. We've lost that ability, but all it takes to reclaim it is to take a cold shower every day.

The result of your investment, the sacrifice of your comfort within the shower, is extraordinary. Yes, it's going to give you a lot more energy. Yes, your heart rate will go down. Yes, it's going to bring all the oxygen and necessary chemistry to your cells. I know I said all this before, but take it as your mantra! After forty-three years of training, I am still reminding myself how good this is, how well it works. You're also going to have a better life because with that energy comes electricity, and your whole body will feel it. It's amazing! You will learn how to command and connect with your body much better because the right chemistry is the conductor of our mind, of the neurology of our brain. The cold is merciless but righteous. It will show you the way.

After ten days of cold showers, you're going to become addicted to it because it feels so good afterward. And you will have that sense of control when you turn the dial. The deeper parts of your physiology suddenly open up, which they have to do because the water really is freezing, and it impacts your body powerfully. But then the deeper parts of your physiology begin to work and meet each other in peace. The cold only shows us whether or not our inner power is present and within our control because we do it consciously. Gradually, more and more, you feel into the cold, and it becomes the teacher. Cold is a stressor, so if you are able to get into the cold and control your body's response to it, you will be able to control stress. Stress comes in many forms, but in the end, you experience it on a biological, cellular level. You can learn to control it by going gradually into the cold and following your feelings. Within ten days, you will see that you are very able to control the stress of the cold. You have to take a shower anyway, right? So, it's very simple. Just end up cold. A minute or two, tops. And then, if you wish, after the ten days—once your body has reconditioned itself—you can increase the exposure.

The control you will gain won't be limited to your body's response to the cold though. It can be applied to stress in any form, be it heat, emotion, work, frustration with the traffic, relationships, whatever. Because the cold is merciless but righteous, we can learn from it. And what it shows us is that we have an innate capacity to deal with stress. It's been lost, yes, but we can regain it within ten days. Ten days! This power is knocking at your door, and it's your choice whether or not to answer. What do you want? Do you want to learn to deal with stress, or do you want to continue suffering? This method is very simple, very accessible, and endorsed by science. Many thousands of people have benefitted from it. Anybody can do it, and there is no dogma, only acceptance. Only freedom.

After you take a cold shower, you'll not only feel like you have more energy, but you will also feel more at rest. Because the brain and the heart are connected neurologically, your decreased heart rate affects your mood, lessening your anxiety. In peace and at rest, your brain begins to "cool down," and blood slowly flows deeper into it. If that blood reaches the limbic system, it is possible to achieve a level of deep meditation that only seasoned mindfulness practitioners of many years have been known to realize. In my experience, a one-minute cold shower every day can deliver you to the same realm. That is power of the mind opening up, of learning how to control the blood flow into the deeper parts of the brain. Those parts of modern man's brain receive less blood flow than those of our prehistoric ancestors, and while those deeper parts survive, they don't flourish. We can't feel it, and it doesn't affect our consciousness. We have to sit still and meditate for hours to get the blood flowing into those deeper realms. Or, conversely, we can take a cold shower.

A cold shower a day, that's the one. That's the ticket to this ride.

In February 2018, I participated in a very interesting study conducted by Wayne State University's School of Medicine in Detroit, Michigan.[4] Professors Otto Muzik and Vaibhav Diwadkar conducted brain scans while exposing seventy-four subjects to ice-cold water over the course of three days. Each of the subjects wore a perfusion vest through which cold water was pumped continuously. The idea was to monitor brain activity and measure differences in the subjects' skin temperature relative to each exposure. Not surprisingly, the skin temperature of the other seventy-three subjects decreased every time the cold water was pumped in. Logical, no? But it is only logical if we accept it as so, if we believe we are limited in our potential. That is the paradigm. I call it "the disconnection" because we do not know the power of our minds.

THE WIM HOF WAY TO GET WARM

Are you one of those people who feels cold all the time? Would you like to be able to warm your body even when you don't have access to an external heat source? If so, the following exercise can be done to activate brown fat tissue (or brown adipose tissue — BAT), which is capable of energy combustion, and your intercostal muscles. The intercostal muscles are several groups of muscles that run between the ribs and help move the chest wall during respiration. Activating them also generates heat.

Do as follows:

1 Sit down.
2 Inhale slowly and deeply five or six times, letting your breath go naturally each time.
3 Inhale fully.
4 Relax to exhale.
5 Inhale fully.
6 Hold your breath, for no more than five seconds.
7 Tense your upper-back muscles and chest while you hold your breath — but don't tense the head. Keep your jaw relaxed.
8 Let go.

With practice, you will feel the heat flowing down from your neck to your whole body. Everybody is different, but with practice, you will feel the heat coming from inside your body. This is what I did to maintain my core body temperature during the experiments at Wayne State — but please do not try such experiments at home!

By employing a deep breathing technique that effectively activated my intercostal muscles (those located between the ribs), I was able to generate enough heat on the first day to maintain my core body temperature. We'll get to intentional breathing in the next chapter. But when it was my turn to don the vest on the third day, I was instructed to participate passively. No muscle contractions or deep breathing, though I had done my breathing exercises in the morning, as I do every morning. But those things can mess up the imaging in the scan and require that the entire experiment be redone. All I could use in this situation was my mind. And when I did nothing with my mind, my skin temperature dropped like everyone else's. I wasn't sure, exactly, what to do. I had always just followed my intuition and my instincts and learned, in nature, what to do and did it. But in nature, you don't think too much about what you're doing, you just do it. It's instinctive. So that morning, I was sitting in my hotel room, looking out my window over Detroit, and thinking, *How do I show it? How do I show a complete difference from those other seventy-three people?* None of them had been able to influence the temperature of their skin during cold-water exposure by using their mind, demonstrating top-down control of their autonomic functions.

So I asked myself, *What did you do on Mount Everest? What did you do in the icy waters beyond the Polar Circle? What did you do always in the cold? You trusted yourself. You believed in your heart that you could do it, and with that state of mind, you went into those challenges with confidence and succeeded. Why shouldn't I be able to do that today?* I saw that it's all a state of mind, and that confidence is a form of trust. It's like a bet you place on yourself. You tell your body what to do, and your body echoes back and says, *yes*. Mind and body are in sync. After all these years, this was quite an epiphany.

In the morning, I did my breathing exercises. Later, when I put on the vest, my skin temperature did not decrease with exposure. It was like I was impervious to it. I had increased my skin temperature by 1 degree because I programmed it with my mind. I didn't move, breathe deeply, or contract my muscles. I didn't do anything except focus my mind and let go. It's something that, with practice and commitment, anybody can do. Just sit with yourself, exclude the world and its worries, and have a clear picture in your mind of the goal you intend to accomplish. Let whatever images and thoughts pass freely and then fall away whilst you are reaching your depth. It is alignment without words but instead with your feelings. There is a strong moment of recognition, as real confidence is not a thought but a feeling from the depth. The method is based on the principle that the power of the mind works in connection with the body to impact human capability in a profound way. It's important to understand that programming in and of itself is something we are each already doing on a daily basis, yet unconsciously. We realize the power of these assumptions when we go into the ice. This helps train the muscle of belief, belief in what we are capable of, which allows us to have confidence in our hearts.

By the time the experiment was completed, I didn't care much about the outcome anymore. But when the professors analyzed the data, they were astonished. They had never seen anything like it before. I had successfully raised my skin temperature by 1 degree and maintained it while being exposed to repeated cycles of cold and warm water. My temperature never changed. That's the power of the mind when it has been awakened by the cold and the breath.

With depression approaching epidemic proportions in the world, new nonpharmaceutical solutions are needed. Brain scans from the Wayne State study demonstrated that I was able to activate parts of my brain at will that had been thought to be inaccessible to humans. This offers a new perspective on how we might be able to deal with psychosis, fear, anxiety, depression, or bipolar disorder independent of drugs.

In nature, it is not only the physically weak but the mentally weak that get eaten. Now we have created this modern society in which we have every comfort, yet we are losing our ability to regulate our mood, our emotions. In the February 2018 issue of *NeuroImage*, professors Muzik and Diwadkar wrote, "We found compelling evidence of the key components of the autonomous processes of the brain related to mood regulation."[5] In plain speak, that's emotion. Now we've found the way to tap into that area and learn to regulate our mood, to regulate our emotional state, whatever you want to call it. It turns out that we are innately capable of dealing with emotion on a conscious level. We are free.

It is important to recognize the gravity of this discovery. It's reminiscent of the fable about the wise men coming together and asking, "What do we do about the soul, since people have made such a mess out of it?" "Put it on the highest of mountains!" one man says. But the people crawl up the mountains like ants, find the soul, and make it a trophy. So the wise men decree, "Put it at the bottom of the deepest seas!" But the people build underwater vessels and dive down under. They find the thing and bring it to the surface and put it in a museum. So the wise men say, "Put it beyond the farthest planet!" But the people build spacecrafts and venture off and find it. They bring it back and make warfare over it. The wise men are confounded because none of them knows where to put the soul. And then one stands up and says, "I've got it! Put it in the people themselves since they never look there."

That's exactly where it is. The soul resides within us. It is within our reach if we know where to look for it. And now we found a shortcut into the deepest parts of the brain, which is the seat of the mind, the soul. It's amazing, and it makes you *feel* amazing because we are amazing beings, but we have to live up to it. We need to use this power for good.

Eradicating cardiovascular disease and positively affecting mental health–care outcomes are, undeniably, applications of the technique that can benefit the greater good. It is accessible, effective, and 100 percent free. We have identified the key components of the autonomous processes in the brain—those outside of our will—and have learned to access them. Those processes are within our will, and with that, our perspective on the human capacity to deal with mood regulation, depression, trauma, and fear must change in accordance. This is the way nature meant for us to be. We have become estranged and alienated from nature, which is why we've lost our innate capacity to enter into our own brains. Humans did not evolve over millions of years to arrive at a lump of meat inside our skulls over which we can control only certain parts. That's nonsense. We can control way more than that. And a lot of that control has to do with emotion, with feeling, with the purpose of life. It starts with the breath and controlling the life-force through breathing. Without the breath, we are nothing, but by controlling it, we are able to access the neurology of our consciousness, our perception. And ten days of cold showers enables us to reregulate the blood flow into the depths of our brains and unlock their true potential. Our brains become one with the life-force, with the blood flow and the breath, and change the chemistry. Suddenly we are able to descend into the deeper parts of ourselves at will because it's all connected. The will is a neurological muscle, but if the biochemistry isn't right, it's not able to do very much.

It's no different from not being able to run well when your muscles are sore. There's nothing wrong with you, per se, and you're not lax. You're not able to run well because you are sore and, thus, your biochemistry is off. Where our mind goes, blood flows. Our society today has us living in a narrowed narrative, and therein we get conditioned. Our brains are cycling through the same thought patterns incessantly, which causes stress and deprives the rest of the brain of the proper flow of blood. As a result, our brains aren't able to function optimally. Our will, which is expressed through neurotransmitters, is not able to enter into a suboptimal biochemistry, into a compromised biological or chemical environment.

It's mind over matter. What we always thought of as abstract or beyond our reach is attainable. But you don't actually have to think about it. Just take the damn cold showers, and you will regain the innate capacity to control your vascular system from the top down. My brain scans demonstrated that it is possible to enter into the deepest part of the brain. We can access and activate our limbic system, which governs memory and emotion. We can also access the brain stem and, connected to that, the periaqueductal gray hemisphere, which is believed to govern the brain's transmission of pain signals.[6] When this neurological channeling is reestablished, it enables us to endure pain by releasing the natural opioids—endocannabinoids—in our brain. These natural chemicals deliver a feeling of euphoria to the body, even under stress, which is exactly the way I felt at Wayne State. I felt no cold at all. I felt no stress. Instead I felt warm. I felt great.

The Wayne State study is the first step in validating this method as a natural remedy for people with health conditions. It's like a fisherman coming back, pulling up his nets, and finding them full of fish. My heart is full. And the beautiful thing is that it's only the beginning. I lost my first wife to suicide in 1995. We had four children together, and she jumped from eight stories up. I was powerless there. She had been suffering for quite some time, and all the injections and pills and therapists in the world couldn't help her. They only made things worse. She jumped after kissing the kids goodbye, and the emotional imprint that formed as a result is deeply rooted within the drive I had, and still have, to develop a means first to survive in the world with four kids and then, in time, to heal. It's like a scar that fades somewhat but is always there. Driven by emotional loss, a broken heart, and having four children and no money, I was highly motivated to make a change,

It's fun to get into the cold with friends!

to offer an alternative solution for those afflicted with mental illness. Now, a quarter century later, we are getting to some answers.

I found those answers in nature. This is an innate power we all possess. It's been conditioned out of us and reinforced by an education system that isn't focused on happiness, strength, health, or a deeper control of ourselves. Do you know what a happy person needs? Nothing. Because he is happy. That is what I want to give to my children, to the beloveds around me, to all the living beings around me. I want to be happy, and I want the same for you. We are all connected by nature. The trees exhale oxygen, and we exhale CO_2. We nourish each other. We are one.

Again, the cold is merciless, but it is absolutely righteous. It goes past the mind, past the conditioning, past all comfort-zone behaviorism, past our weakness, and makes us strong. After millions of years of evolutionary development, it returns us to our optimal condition. We put on clothes and live in climate-controlled environments and lead largely sedentary lives, but inside, biologically, we are still like any other mammal. It is very simple, and now, through science — with data — we have proven that we possess the innate capacity to control our mind. The applications are limitless — inflammation, chronic pain — it's all within our grasp. We can tackle cardiovascular-related diseases and depression. Wouldn't that be bloody great? And it's much simpler than we thought. All we need to do to begin reclaiming our innate capacity, our inner power, our ability to place mind over matter, and achieve strength, happiness, and sustainable health is to take cold showers. Just a minute or two a day. It's all there for you, and we have proven through science that it works. It just needs awakening. A cold shower a day keeps the doctor away.

WIM HOF METHOD EXPERIMENT #1

ICE-WATER BATH FOR WARMER HANDS AND FEET

Are you someone who suffers from cold hands or feet? If so, try this exercise.[7]

STEP 1 Fill a bucket with one-third ice and two-thirds water.

STEP 2 Redirect your mental focus to your hands (or feet).

STEP 3 Place your hands or feet into the ice bucket.

STEP 4 Hold your hands or feet in the bucket for two minutes. At some point, they should start to feel warm instead of cold.

STEP 5 Remove your hands or feet from the ice bucket, but keep your mental focus on them.

STEP 6 Shake them out several times to encourage the blood flow into your newly awakened extremities.

Your blood vessels constrict in the ice bucket at first. This is a natural protective mechanism. But then they open when your blood reaches 50 degrees Fahrenheit, allowing warm blood to flood into them. You are resetting the physiology in your extremities. People who often complain of cold hands or feet suffer from poor vasoconstriction and dilation. The muscles around the veins in their hands and feet do not function well and need to be retrained. This ice-bucket exercise helps. If you typically have cold hands or feet, try doing this exercise daily. Adaptation occurs rather quickly. After a couple of days of this exercise, you will find that your extremities aren't so cold anymore.

4

BREATHE
MOTHERF*CKER

The first time doctors monitored a group of people I had trained in the method, they observed as these people went minutes without breathing, without air in their lungs. The monitors showed their blood oxygen levels going down dramatically, to saturation numbers like 50 percent, which is normally where people die. But these people were thriving. Do you know why? The biochemistry had changed. And with that spiking of alkalinity, the brain's adrenal axis is activated. That resets the body past its conditioning, beyond its comfort zone, and enables it to withstand and overcome stress.

Crohn's disease, cancer, depression, arthritis, asthma, and bipolar disorder are all caused by deregulation of our immune, endocrine, and hormonal systems through uncontrolled inflammation.[1] Now, by employing these simple breathing techniques, we are able to suppress the inflammatory markers in the blood. I challenge any doctor who remains skeptical, who believes this isn't real, to try it for themselves. We've got strong evidence, and it's been published in the best scientific journals in the world. As you'll see in the chapters to come, we changed the books.

We are able to tap into the autonomic nervous system and suppress inflammation. We can regulate our mood, emotions, body temperature, and more. The breathing exercises employed through the method help clean up the biochemical residue (the undesired by-products of a chemical reaction) in the lymphatic system, the deepest of all bodily systems. All the stressful activities we do in our work and emotional life leave behind a biochemical residue that causes and compounds inflammation in our cells. I am convinced that by changing our biochemistry from acidic to alkaline and cleansing ourselves of biochemical residue, we can eliminate the primary causes of diseases.

While they can have a profound impact on your physical and emotional state, the breathing exercises themselves are actually very simple. It's just thirty or forty deep breaths taken while lying on a sofa or bed, with periods of retention. The location is important. Always do these breathing exercises in a safe environment, never in an environment in which it might be dangerous to faint, like in water. These exercises have a profound effect on the body, especially for those new to the method, and should only be practiced in the way I am about to explain. Okay?

When you breathe in deeply, your diaphragm moves, and that massages your intestines. That's the natural way, though most of us breathe only with our chests and never massage our intestines in that way. But the belly goes up when the diaphragm moves — when the lungs expand — and that's why we call it "belly breathing." Only it's not really the belly; it's the lungs being filled to their utmost capacity. The belly goes up because it needs to make space. Then the upper parts of the lungs get filled up.

The breathing protocol, which is composed of three to four rounds, takes about twenty minutes to complete. The best time to do these breathing exercises is before breakfast because when your stomach is full, all the metabolic activity and all the oxygen are directed to the stomach and block the way. This is logical because digestion is a function of the parasympathetic nervous system, and with the breathing, we are activating our sympathetic nervous system. The breathing ignites the body into an alert state, awakening the nervous system and preparing the body for performance. Eating beforehand can inhibit this physiological reaction.

The technique begins, as I mentioned above, with thirty to forty deep breaths. When you are new to this technique, I advise you to breathe through the nose, as it will give you more control over your body and mind. With more experience, you can breathe in through your mouth or through your nose. It doesn't matter. Don't think too much about it, just bring it in. I prefer to breathe through my mouth, but you should do whatever feels the most comfortable for you. It's about filling the belly and letting it go, like a wave. A wave comes up on the beach, on the shore, and then it recedes. There is a rhythm to it, and so it goes with the breathing. Breathe in fully and then let it go. Here comes the wave again. Follow the breath fully in, then letting go. Fully in, letting go. The mind follows the breath, but don't try to contain the breath in your mind. Let the mind go. The breath is greater, and it brings you further into the depths of yourself, so follow the flow, follow the wave coming in onto the shore, and then let it go. The breath is as big as the ocean. Let it in fully, then let it go. It is the sea itself. It's where we came from, who we are. It is bigger than us because it *is* us. Now go consciously into the breath and let it go. Fully in, letting go, fully in, letting go. Find your rhythm and follow it. While more or less we are the same, everyone's physiology is a little bit different. Everyone has a slightly different rhythm. That doesn't matter though. Just breathe and go with the flow.

Do this thirty times or until you feel lightheaded with a tingling sensation in your arms and hands and a looseness in your body. Breathe into the sensation. Take it up ten more times to forty breaths now, deeply in — feel the breath expanding your belly, chest, head — and then let go. Then fully in again and letting go. Forty times. You can keep count on your fingers or in your mind. By now you should definitely be feeling the lightheadedness, tingling, and looseness I described. Intensify those sensations by breathing into them. Don't worry, it's all okay. You are 100 percent safe. Carbon dioxide is exiting your body, and oxygen is replacing it, making your body more alkaline in the process. It may feel a bit strange or disorienting at first, but it's great for your biochemistry.

The neurological effect is like a tension charge all over the body. So just follow the breath, and you will feel the charge.

Now we are going to bring the consciousness in. Yes, the breath is a door. It leads to corridors that take us deep within ourselves. We begin doing this by stopping the breath while the body is alkalized. After you let the fortieth breath go, stop after the exhalation. Holding your breath here will be fairly easy because your newfound alkalinity lessens the body's need for oxygen. You may be surprised to learn that you can easily hold your breath and go without any air in your lungs for thirty seconds, a minute, even a minute and a half at this point. You're the alchemist now. You're the one who's doing it, and you're in control.

What happens in your body now is a chain of chemical reactions. The brain requires oxygen to function, of course, but the trigger for breathing is an acidic state, which you have eliminated by becoming alkalized through breathing. Nothing wrong is happening in your body, but your primitive, reptilian brain doesn't know that. It says, "There is no oxygen." And while there is no immediate need for oxygen when your body is in this alkalized state, the primitive brain reacts by activating the adrenal axis and resetting the body to a physiological state in which we have a neurological control and

A group breathing exercise at the WHM Center in Stroe, Netherlands

connection with everything inside. That's the way man existed in nature originally—alert, fully present, and just being.

When you feel a real urge to breathe again, go ahead. Breathe in once, inhaling fully, and then, when your lungs are full, stop again. You are now consciously tapping into the endocrine system and igniting the nervous system, releasing hormones and unblocking energy. Advancing in the technique, you may encounter lights, visions. It's up to you how far you want to go with this because the feeling can be rather intense. But don't hold your breath so long that you pass out. Just breathe in as soon as you feel you have to. Remember to always follow the breath as a guide and not to force it. Letting go is the key.

What I believe you're doing is influencing your pineal gland, the *epiphysis cerebri*, known in ancient literature as the third eye or the seat of the soul. The blood flows there, and so does electricity. And as the body's electricity activates the hormones in the pineal gland, images and experiences locked deep within your subconscious mind enter your consciousness. Because we are present in this moment with our ego, our awareness, we are suddenly able to access these visions and feelings that are normally locked away from us, and it's beautiful. When we do this exercise as a group, it seems to amplify this effect. The simple act of breathing together creates a bond. Hearing others breathing open us up to the simple vulnerability of human life. People start to laugh, or cry, sometimes with no real connection to a particular story, as they access the emotions stored in their bodies. The experience can trigger lights or familiar faces, shapes and images to enter into your consciousness. Strange sensation or ringing in your ears. My belief is that it's like a dream state, the kind we can usually only achieve during the REM cycle, in which dimethyltryptamine (DMT), a powerful psychoactive chemical, is released naturally into the bloodstream. It's a true natural high, and it is at this moment that anxiety and the pain of trauma fall away from your consciousness because you have freed yourself from it by consciously manipulating the biochemistry and electricity in your brain.

That is conscious alchemy. That's the way you bring your ego to an egoless state of being, into the gold of your own corona, the uninhibited energy around your head that enables the whole of your being to transcend and become holy, in a sense. That may sound far-out to you, but it's true. We are the alchemists, and we are built to be in command of our own soul, light, spirit, and life. This is just one way in. Your way, my way, however we arrive there, we all come to the same thing in the end, which is love, you know? Just breathe and retain your breath in the manner I have described, and the rest will take care of itself naturally. When the breath gets into the brain's electricity, it affects our neurological activity in a profound way. All your brain needs is a little biochemical nourishment. If we provide it with that nourishment with the breath and then follow the natural flow of our inner development, we will find that it leads toward freedom.

This is only the beginning of your journey to unlock the unlimited power of your mind. This is just round number one. With further training and practice, you will eventually be able to be at one with the deepest part of your brain and reap far-reaching benefits for your health and happiness. Our thinking brain is only a way station. At any given moment, our brains are regulating our body with thousands of processes, systems that we are not consciously tapped into. Consciously influencing the deepest part of your brain or blood flow is a different type of consciousness. You have to train in this. Be still, and breathe. That is where the depth is gained. This is the promise, and our challenge is to live up to it. We can live in sensitive connection with our most vulnerable souls and become the enlightened, radiant beings we were meant to be. It all begins with forty breaths.

Now we go and do the breathing sequence once again. Round two. Forty breaths followed by a hold after the last exhalation, and you will notice that you are able to go longer without breathing this time because your body has become even more alkaline. This increased alkalinity also increases the amount of time it takes for your body to build up an acidic state again, which is what triggers the urge to breathe. So, during round number two, you will notice you can go a little longer without air in the lungs.

When you feel the urge to breathe again, take it all the way in and hold it for ten to fifteen seconds. You may at this time begin to see even more of what's happening within you, and the sensation you will feel is pure bliss. The Hindus call this feeling *satchitananda*, with *sat* meaning "energy" or "truth," *chit* meaning "intelligence," and *ananda* meaning "bliss."[2] That's the trinity of our spirit, of our soul's purest expression. *The Vedas* were written thousands of years ago, but their truth endures. You will experience satchitananda here in your second round of breathing because it reflects the blood, electricity, and light rushing through you.

After this second held inhale of fifteen seconds or so, it's time for round three. Don't worry too much about how long you can hold your breath. If you are dealing with a lot of inflammation, you may need to breathe sooner. In this way, the breath is like a mirror that shows you the state you are in. Everybody's experience with the breathing is a little bit different, but the universal characteristics are that with each successive round you feel stronger, lighter, and more at peace. Every round sends more blood and electricity into the brain. Every round reactivates the adrenal axis. And if you do four rounds, as I recommend, you'll be ready for the day because you will have seen the light. More than that, you will have *become* the light re-balancing of parasympathetic/sympathetic nervous system. On top of that, four rounds will ensure that your blood is within the optimum pH range. These factors have many benefits, not only for your physical health but also spiritually. Achieving that biochemical and hormonal balance increases your energy, boosts your performance, and lowers your stress levels. All after just four rounds of breathing.

WHM PROTOCOL: BASIC BREATHING EXERCISE

Before engaging with this breathing technique, remember to be mindful. Listen to your body and learn from the signals your body and mind send you while you are doing the exercises. Use those signals as personal feedback about the effect of the exercises on your body and mind, and adjust them as needed to find what works best for you.[3]

STEP 1 Sit in a meditation posture, lying down, or whichever way is most comfortable for you, in a quiet and safe environment. Make sure you can expand your lungs freely without feeling any constriction.

STEP 2 Close your eyes and try to clear your mind. Be conscious about your breath and try to fully connect with it. Take thirty to forty deep breaths in through the nose or mouth. Fill up your belly, your chest, all the way up to your head. Don't force the exhale. Just relax and let the air out. Fully in, letting go.

STEP 3 At the end of the last breath, draw the breath in once more and fill the lungs to maximum capacity without using any force. Then relax to let the air out. Hold the breath until you feel the urge to breathe again. This is called the retention phase.

STEP 4 When you feel the urge to breathe, take one deep breath in and hold it for ten to fifteen seconds. This is called the recovery breath.

STEP 5 Let your breath go and start with a new round. Fully in, letting go. Repeat the full cycle three to four times.

After having completed this breathing exercise, take your time to enjoy the feeling. With repeated practice, this protocol becomes more and more like a meditation.

Once you have a little experience with the basic breathing exercise, try this additional technique: In round 2, step 4, try "squeezing" the breath to your head when you take your recovery breath. You do this by tensing your pelvic floor and directing that sense of tension to the core of your body and up to your head, while keeping the rest of your body relaxed. You should feel a sense of pressure in your head. Then relax everything when you exhale.

But that's not all this breathing method can do. In January 2014, I led a group of twenty-six people trained in the method up Tanzania's Mount Kilimanjaro with a goal of reaching the summit in three days. None of these people were experienced alpinists, and some of them suffered from debilitating illnesses and diseases, such as multiple sclerosis, rheumatoid arthritis, and metastasized cancer. In the interest of avoiding acute mountain sickness (AMS), which can be fatal in extreme cases, most people who attempt to climb the highest mountain on the African continent do so gradually over the course of five days or more. They do this so that their bodies can acclimatize to the increasing altitude on their way to the mountain's summit, which sits more than nineteen thousand feet above sea level (to avoid AMS, it is recommended that climbers ascend no more than one thousand feet per day). But armed with my breathing method and deeply motivated mindset but little else, including cold weather gear (though we did take some with us as a precaution), we headed off knowing that we would reach our goal. All the physiologists, doctors, and alpine experts I consulted said that what I was trying to do was irresponsible. People were going to get sick, they said. Some might even die. But up we went anyway, doing our specific high-altitude breathing technique and reached the summit in just forty-four hours. That's twenty-eight hours less than our initial three-day goal! We defied the wisdom of the experts. And when we came back down the mountain, the critics were silent. A year later we returned to Kilimanjaro and reached the summit in just thirty-six hours. And the year after that, we did it in just over twenty-eight hours. Unbelievable.

In a letter to the editor of *Wilderness and Environmental Medicine*, Drs. Hopman and Buijze, who supervised the 2014 expedition, wrote, "The group appears to have broken new medical ground, utilizing a new method to largely prevent, and as needed, reverse, symptoms of acute mountain sickness. . . . In comparison with previous studies, this report may suggest that acclimatization, as well as AMS symptom relief, can be safely accelerated."[4]

IN CASE OF ALTITUDE HEADACHES

Headaches are the first sign of altitude sickness; a headache indicates that the brain is being deprived of oxygen. This exercise fuels your brain with oxygen again and should bring instant relief.

1 Slow down your pace.
2 Breathe in fully and relax to exhale ten times.
3 Stand still or sit. Make sure you are in a secure position.
4 Breathe in fully, hold your breath for five seconds, and try squeezing or redirecting the breath to your head.

5 Let go.
6 Repeat these steps until you sense that the headache has disappeared.

BREATHING EXERCISE WHILE WALKING AT HIGH ALTITUDE

1 Consciously breathe more than you feel you need to.
2 Focus on your breath. Feel yourself breathing as you move.
3 Synchronize your breath and your pace so you can get into a cadence. Find your own rhythm without forcing it.

RESTING BREATHING EXERCISE TO ADJUST TO AN ALTITUDE GREATER THAN THIRTEEN THOUSAND FEET

This exercise can help you to forestall the potentially dangerous symptoms caused by a low oxygen level in your body that you may encounter if climbing or visiting somewhere where the altitude exceeds thirteen thousand feet. Please do not rely on this exercise to prevent altitude sickness symptoms without the proper supervision or experience. The best way to safely learn it is to participate in one of our expeditions. See "Further Reading" for more information. It is helpful to use a saturation meter to measure your blood oxygen level when doing this.

1 Wake up four to four-and-a-half hours after you went to sleep.
2 Do the Basic Breathing Exercise until your saturation meter reads a minimum of 95 to 100 percent saturation.
3 Practice the breathing exercises for at least a half hour.
4 Go back to sleep.

Among the many health-beneficial applications of the breathing method is its ability to regulate that which causes disease, namely inflammation. German physiologist Otto H. Warburg was awarded the Nobel Prize in 1931 for discovering that low oxygen is a characteristic of cancer cells. So on top of its manifold benefits, this breathing method may also help you ward off illness. As we will discuss in later chapters, one of the causes of inflammation is biochemical imbalance. We may be able to survive and function more or less normally for a while when our biochemistry isn't right, but eventually ailments will manifest. They arrive in the form of autoimmune diseases, cancer, depression. And they come because our biochemical nature is out of balance.

We have to quit with this comfort-zone behaviorism and get back to our innermost needs. How do you do that? By breathing. Breathing the right way, massaging our intestines, becoming alkaline. These breathing exercises are partially based on ancient practices, but they have been brought up-to-date with our modern way of living, the modern condition of our neurology. While physically, humans are more or less the same as we were during the middle ages, our brains process so much more stimuli than they did back then. To function optimally, the brain requires a different biochemistry. With this breathing method, we can both regulate and manipulate our biochemistry. This isn't speculative, but proven. The science is clear. It works. People come up to me with questions like, "Should I breathe through the nose?" or "The diaphragm this or that," and I just say, "Yeah, breathe, motherfuckers! Don't think, just do it! Get into the depth of your own lungs!" Because all you have to do to reap the benefit of the method is to do it. You will feel transformed in minutes, after a few rounds of breathing. So get out of your mind and get into your breath because the breath is the life-force. Not your mind, the breath. Follow your breath, and it will lead you anywhere in your brain — thus the mind — that you want to go.

WIM HOF METHOD EXPERIMENT #2

EXTENDING YOUR RETENTION TIME

You can control your biochemistry with your breath. Don't believe me? Well try this:

STEP 1 Breathe normally, then exhale fully, hold your breath out, and time how long you can hold it for.

STEP 2 Do the same thing after taking thirty deep breaths, relaxing the air out on the exhale.

Big difference, huh? The reason why you can hold your breath for so much longer after taking thirty deep breaths is because the deep breathing temporarily changes the ratio between carbon dioxide and oxygen in your blood. Because your breathing reflex is correlated to the amount of carbon dioxide in your blood and you just exhaled a lot of carbon dioxide, you can hold your breath for longer. Carbon dioxide is an acid, and the breathing causes your pH level to increase, bringing your body into a temporarily alkaline state.

Within twenty or twenty-five minutes of doing these breathing exercises, you will be able to experience the unlimited power of the breath within your mind, and you will not only feel its intensity but see real, tangible results. When we consciously change our biochemistry through breathing, we make our bodies happier, stronger, and healthier. How simple! Do you see how simple it all is? All of these complicated matters that clutter our minds are meaningless. All of that stress just takes us further away from nature, but the breath will take you back. It will forge that deeper connection we have lost. Is that not what you want for yourself, your kids, and everybody around you?

So many in the world today are consumed with artificial desires. We grasp at imaginary straws. We work harder and harder and stress ourselves out to achieve more and more, but to what end? So we can become lawyers and businesspeople? So we can make lots of money to buy a big house or a fancy car but that can't buy us happiness or health? I saw too much of that misery, which is why I withdrew from that world a long time ago. And it's also why I began to think, *What is the soul? Where is it?* Well, I found it first in the cold and then in the breath that followed. There's nothing mystical or abstract about it. It's physical. Your breath is your life-force, right here, right now. It could not be any simpler. Just breathe and reclaim your soul.

I developed these exercises after going into the cold because the first thing you do when you encounter the cold is gasp. It's like being reborn. Breath is the life-force. In this case the breath serves as a catalyst. You bring the air deeper into your lungs, and with that air entering deeper into your tissues, your body's chemistry begins to change. It gets invigorated by good oxygen, good nutrients. Good vitamins get absorbed into your cells, and that creates more energy. That's why we do the breathing first, before going into the cold. The breathing generates heat through the intercostal muscles, and it also increases your pain tolerance. You do keep on following the breath with your attention once you enter the water, maintaining the connection with the brain. This is conscious breathing, which is different from the three or four rounds with retention that we do while lying or sitting down in a safe place. But you'd better learn to silence your ongoing thoughts when you enter the water because they're not going to help you there. Just clear your mind, be determined, and trust your breath because the breath goes everywhere—inside and out.

These understandings, achieved through rigorous experimentation, informed the development and refinement of the breathing technique, but only after I learned how to deal with the cold's aggressive impact on my body. I did this by consciously changing my biochemistry. The energy of the cold's impact met the energy generated by my deep breathing, and the effect was transformative. It wasn't long before I could stay in icy water for hours. I could stay outside in the cold all night long because I learned how to regulate my energy through my breath and my consciousness. You can do it too.

Consciousness, awareness, perception—we'll get back to all that—but now we are into the cold again. The cold's immediate impact on the body can feel a bit painful, like pricking needles, but after a minute or so, when your natural opioids and cannabinoids kick in, the discomfort subsides and is replaced by a sense of euphoria. You get ten times more energy back as the blood flow begins to run through your body, and it makes your mind still.

Afterward you will see that your skin is all red and beautifully colored because the skin is alive. We always have it covered with clothes, which de-stimulates it, but cold is able to reinvigorate it. The best thing you can do for your skin is to go into cold water—not shockingly, but gradually; I'm sixty-one years old, and I still have skin like a baby's.

People today—supposedly health-conscious people—are so caught up in the latest nutrition, fitness, or spiritual trends because they are still seeking. But I found what I was looking for in the cold water and in the breath. I found stillness of the mind, peace, and positive energy. The cold exists beyond our thoughts, and if we go into it gradually—by increasing incrementally, say, the length of our cold shower each day—we find that within ten days, a cascade of things begins to happen. First, your heart rate goes down, which means less stress. Then your vascular system wakes up and optimizes to its natural condition. You feel more alive. When you add the breathing practice to your regular routine, you can feel results immediately in the form of more energy, a sense of well-being. Alkalizing your body with the breath will start to reduce the inflammation that brings you pain. Both the breathing exercises and the cold train the vascular system and impact the biochemistry, although the cold is more about the vascular system and the breath is more about the biochemistry. The breathing also regulates the sympathetic and parasympathetic nervous systems. This is integral for overall health and well-being. This is alchemy.

This book is about showing you how to tap into your long-dormant physiology and to return your body and mind to the state nature originally intended for them to be in. The methods described here will enable you to tap into not only your five senses, but also extra senses you may not know you have, which we'll get into in chapter 12. For now, just continue on with the cold showers and practicing the breathing techniques, as they work wonders. But simultaneously, you'll be building a totally new physiological perspective. And while the cold and the breath are working their beautiful magic on your body and brain, providing numerous physical and mental benefits, these practices also allow you to cross a new threshold and access the power of your brain, the seat of the mind. More on that in the next chapter.

It's time to embrace our inner mammals before it's too late, before we lose our connection to our inner nature forever. It's all there for us. Saying "a cold shower a day keeps the doctor away" or "breathe, motherfuckers" are oversimplifications, I'll admit, but we are dealing with the quality of our lives. It's all biochemistry. Through the breath, we become alkaline and oxygenated and become more able to regulate our nervous system. Through the cold, we are able to activate the blood flow and get it within our willful control. We gain this control from the mind. Yes, the mind can be corrupted by thoughts and ego, as I have explained, but those things are separate from the body, separate from the sacred parts of who and what we are, and separate from the soul.

HOW TO CURE A HANGOVER IN TWENTY MINUTES

If you do the breathing techniques described in this book, you'll know how to deal with toxic substances in the body, including the dreaded hangover. Anyone who has ever overindulged on red wine, beer, whiskey, tequila, or whatever and has woken up feeling like holy hell knows the pain and discomfort of the hangover. There are all sorts of pills, powders, potions, and other concoctions on the market that claim to cure hangovers, but none of them are as effective as twenty to twenty-five minutes of my breathing method.

Don't believe me? Then take my daughter Laura. When Laura was twenty-three years old, she was pursuing double master's degrees with a laser focus. She rarely drank and never smoked and was instead fully committed to her work. She spent her days bent over her computer, banging away at her theses. But one night, she was at a party and cut loose a bit. She drank way more than she was used to and woke up feeling horrible. She called me up and said, "Dad, I can't work. I don't feel good. I've got a terrible headache."

Mind you that to this point, Laura had never done my breathing or engaged with my method in any way. Children don't listen to their fathers, to their parents, like that because they don't want to yield to their authority. But on this morning, it was her hangover, not me, who was the authority. It was something she'd never dealt with before, but there it was — the residue of the red, red wine. And Laura was struggling.

"Listen," I said. "You have seen me doing this breathing all your life. So, for God's sake or for yours, do the breathing and just try it out. It really works!" Naturally she resisted, but eventually, perhaps out of desperation, she relented and began to do it. Thirty deep breaths, exhale fully, hold, inhale, hold, repeat. And you know what? Within twenty minutes, her headache was gone, and she was able to work again. Happy days!

How did it work? It's simple, really. The breathing alkalizes the blood, which eliminates the acidity caused by toxic substances like alcohol. I learned this myself firsthand after enjoying, on occasion, a few too many glasses of red wine. Twenty to twenty-five minutes, and it's over, you're done. Easy peasy.

I was happy to help my daughter, of course, but I was also pleased because it was the first time in her entire life that she had taken on something I was doing. I had always been the weird dad, you see, the dad who would show up at school wearing open sandals in midwinter, with snow on the ground, and do handstands in the courtyard. The other parents would smoke their cigarettes, stare, and sneer at me. "He's crazy," they'd say. "He's not normal." Oh, but it's normal to smoke poison and talk about somebody else like that? The children just wanted me to be normal, a regular papa like the others. They were embarrassed by me sometimes. But I was not normal then just as I am not normal now. I was searching for something else, something bigger, and I didn't care much about the perception of others. That was hard for the children to understand, but in time, all four of the kids I had with Olaya came around to my way of thinking. They all work with me now. It's a family-run business, you know. I get to see and interact with my kids, who are now adults, every day. It's wonderful. And for Laura, it all started with a hangover.

5 THE POWER OF THE MIND

There are three pillars to the Wim Hof Method. The first two are the cold and the breath. The third pillar of the method is mindset. We call this pillar "commitment" in our training programs because you must have the right mindset to make the commitment to go against your ego and take the damn shower, to just breathe. You could also call this pillar the power of the mind. It includes the idea of will and the power to imagine, to meditate, to visualize — the power to send your attention to any part of your body, to observe any bodily process. We have this power. We look to the ancient yogis and shamans for the secrets of mind power, but it is simpler than all of that. It is all right here for us, proven by science. Scientific studies and personal experience give us the confidence we need to do the method. They gave me the confidence to continue on my mission.

The Wayne State University findings were not only spectacular, they marked a real breakthrough in our scientific understanding of how we can control our minds to consciously alter our biochemistry. How does it work? When you go into the cold, you're not thinking anymore, you're just doing. Then, suddenly, the body's autonomic processes take over. We have to go deeper to cut through our conditioning and gain control of those processes.

The body's default mode is survival. It does what it needs to do to keep its vital organs functioning, and that's precisely what it does when it is confronted by an environmental stressor like the cold. The cold is a teacher. It's merciless. You don't picnic when you go into the cold. You don't think about your mortgage or your kid's braces or your divorce; you just survive. You reactivate the deepest part of your brain. This is what I've been showing through the method, how to do that, moving beyond our conditioning and the established neurological pathways to reawaken what has been long dormant within us.

Suddenly your consciousness syncs with your biochemistry, and you can naturally address what ails you—anxiety, fear, depression, what have you. With the flow of blood delivering oxygen and nutrients into the deepest parts of your brain, you feel stillness, you feel pure energy, you feel the true power of your mind. That's the way we should feel every day, and we can—not only be happy, strong, and healthy, but imbued with purpose and a sense of adventure. Your soul comes alive. That's what the cold water does. It teaches you not only how to survive, but to thrive. It's all within your control.

It took me many years to get to the point where the scientific community looked upon me and my methods as anything more than a curiosity, if not a sideshow, so the gradual acceptance and ultimate validation these studies engender have gone a long way toward legitimizing what we are doing. It would be easy for me to say that this validation isn't necessary, that I've known the truth of it all along, and that the proof of the method's effectiveness can be found among the many thousands it has benefited. But in an effort to reach as many people as possible, to help people on a worldwide scale—which is my goal—the support of the scientific community is invaluable.

Among others, professors and immunologists have taken up our cause. Immediately after the initial results from a study I did with Radboud University Medical Center were published, Frits Muskiet, a professor of clinical chemistry at the University of Gronigen, went on national Dutch radio and said that they had "put their finger on practically all diseases of prosperity. Our bodies," Muskiet explained, "continually combat and destroy infections. The body should be in balance, but it isn't. Because of our current lifestyles, we live with permanent low levels of infection. You could say that we are chronically infected, but because the infection is so low, we don't feel it at all. . . . The experimental group has shown us that it is possible to repress that inflammatory response. I hope that this leads to much more research."[1]

We have shown through scientific evidence and comparative studies that cold exposure, in combination with conscious breathing, meditation, and a positive mental attitude, has far-reaching benefits to human health. Devoted practitioners of the method have been able to reverse diabetes, alleviate the debilitating effects of Parkinson's disease, lose weight, and achieve remarkable athletic feats. But in order to reap the full benefit of the method, you've got to fully commit your mind to it. Tune out distractions. Turn off your television and leave your phone in another room when you begin the breathing exercises each morning. Give yourself enough time that time doesn't factor into your thoughts at all. These twenty to twenty-five minutes a day require your complete attention. The mind is a neurological muscle that is able to influence your body's molecular systems and aid its absorption of oxygen, which creates the energy you want. And if you want this muscle to function optimally, you've got to surrender unconditionally to the experience. You have to really go for it. You have to have the third pillar: confidence, mindset.

This confidence is nothing abstract. I am not talking about believing in something blindly. I am talking about a feeling of focused alignment. Do these techniques and trust in the feeling it gives you. You are exercising the very wiring of your body with the cold and the breath, leading to an ability to activate your body, to fend off stress and execute whatever needs to be done with the power of your mind. You are in charge. Develop confidence and conviction in what you are doing. It is only then that you will be able to connect to your inner power, to your true nature.

To get the most out of the method, you have to mentally invest in it. You have to commit yourself to it fully. Your mindset can powerfully influence your physiology. A 2015 proof-of-principle study added on to the Endotoxin experiment showed that a higher level of optimism related to an even stronger immune response.[2] Your mind is an amazing tool.

A dose of skepticism is healthy, of course, and we have already converted many skeptics into believers. Journalist Scott Carney was sent to Poland by *Playboy* magazine with the express purpose of exposing me as a charlatan. But not only did he leave my training camp as a believer, he ended up writing a bestselling book, *What Doesn't Kill Us*, in which he chronicles his experience with the method culminating in the near-summitting of Kilimanjaro.

Carney's not the only skeptic we've converted. People come to the method for various reasons, some inspired by what I have done, some motivated to change their lives, some still wanting to see if this is all just a bit of hoo-ha. The method stands on its own merits. Whatever it is, I simply want to bring people back to their inner power. What you do with that inner power is your business. It's like coming home to yourself. Set your mind as you please. Do the breathing. See how it feels. Go into the cold. Endeavor to go deep. Remain curious to the experience. Remain open, but commit to it. Be determined.

As the saying goes, "Whether you think you can or you think you can't, you're right." It's a quote that's often attributed to the American automobile manufacturer Henry Ford, who knew a little bit about belief, I'd say, but the message in those words stretches back thousands of years. It's timeless, really. Your mindset, your attitude plays a critical role in determining your success or failure in any endeavor, and these techniques are no exception. I am living proof of their effectiveness, and thousands of others, skeptics included, are as well. And just as there are no atheists in foxholes, there are no non-believers in the ice bath. In fact, just stepping into an ice bath represents, for some, a leap of faith. But when we achieve a state in which there are no thoughts but just feelings, strong feelings, like those at the root of faith, there is only love. And love is like its own life-force; it makes you fly. I'm in love with life every day, and I'm determined to spread my message and let the world know that this kind of love is attainable for everyone. Love for life, love between one another, love for anything that happens — good or bad — because we are precious, amazing beings of infinite potential. Believe it.

Am I crazy? Yes, I'm crazy about life and my wife. I guarantee happiness, strength, and health to all who are close to me because that is what I wish for all my beloveds. It's what I wish for all people, really, anybody alive because I respect life. Life is within me, and I know its purpose, which is to radiate love. If that makes me crazy, so be it. We are kings and queens, and when we wake up to the power within us and we seek to live up to its responsibility, then what else would be very important? What else would make you happy? To own six cars? A big house? Material things are external and have no bearing on the soul. You can only drive one car and occupy one room at a time. But if you seek happiness within your own being, in control over your own life-force, mind, and purpose, nothing else matters. You can be happy unconditionally. That's the kind of happiness I want to give to the people I love because it comes from within. It's already there. The conductor is love, which is the greatest power in the universe because it enables the soul to express itself. Without the soul, there is only darkness, black matter, war. We are the bearers of light, and we have the control through the mind and through the neurology of our heart forging a deeper connection with our brains. That connection is called love, and with this method, we are able to spread it around and heal this world. It's time.

There is no dogma with any of this. It's not religion, it's science. So you can decide for yourself whether or not you want to be happy, strong, and healthy. In the pages that follow, I will explain more of the science behind the findings. But for now, it is enough just to feel and see and believe. What do you want? If you want to be happy, strong, healthy, and in control of your mind, heart, and purpose, you can find all of that within yourself.

In January 2008, I was invited to New York to stand packed in a thousand pounds of ice on the sidewalk outside the Rubin Museum of Art.[3] It was my first visit to the United States, and we were attempting to set a new world record for cold endurance. Twenty teams of cameras descended upon me, and I was to open a new series of events for this museum, which specialized in Himalayan art and culture, with a public demonstration of my technique. They understood it to be based loosely on the ancient Tibetan practice of *tummo*, or inner heat. Lamas are trained in this traditional technique over the course of a lengthy solitary retreat. To prove they have mastered it, they have to dry out a wet sheet with only their body heat while sitting in meditation in the freezing cold Himalayan air. The Rubin Museum billed me as a master, which I suppose I was, but what they did not know is that I had studied under no master in Tibet, Dharamsala, or anywhere else. My teachers were the canals and parks of Amsterdam. That's where I had learned to expose myself to the cold and that's where, in Beatrixpark, I first entered into icy water. Twenty-five years of trial and error, of testing, tweaking, and refining my practice had led me to this point. It was a relatively warm day for January in New York, about 36 degrees Fahrenheit. The wind was blowing through the streets. People gathered around, including media from all over the world, all surveilling me with their electronic eyes as I climbed inside the plexiglass. It was like a circus.

That was the day I met Ken Kamler for the first time. Dr. Kamler is an authority in America, the lead doctor on expeditions up Mount Everest and K2. He is the author of *Doctor on Everest* and *Surviving the Extremes*, two books based on his experiences practicing medicine in extreme environments. That was also the day I first met Kamler's assistant, Granis Stewart, a nurse and free diver, who possessed knowledge of breathing techniques. Both Kamler and Granis had some personal interest in being there, and they monitored my vital signs and body temperature throughout the duration of the attempt.

Just a few months earlier, I had run a full marathon on Mount Everest, at an altitude of about fifteen thousand feet, barefoot for eight hours. As a gesture of goodwill and to wish me good luck, some Tibetans had gifted me a bandana of sorts, a white blessing scarf called a *kata*. I brought the kata to New York with me and, considering the Rubin Museum's specialized focus and hoping it still possessed some magic, wore it around my head.

There was a buzz building among the crowd, and I felt that excitement, but I didn't let it affect me. I knew what I was doing and what was going to happen because I had programmed it. I just stood there in the ice and did my thing like I always do in nature. I shut out the outside world and focused my energies within, and while my core body

Here I am packed in ice outside of the Rubin Museum of Art in New York City

temperature gradually dropped by 10 degrees to a level that would be fatal to an average person, I was then able to raise it by 6 degrees with the power of my mind. This astonished Dr. Kamler and his team, not to mention the live television audience, but I knew that by programming the neurology of my mind, I could make my body more active inside. I could increase the amount of metabolic activity going on and also activate all kinds of hormones to generate heat from within. It's a sequence of things, a chain reaction, and it makes your body so strong. You activate the brain's adrenal axis and become warmer in the presence of cold, cooler in the presence of heat, and more receptive to optimal oxygen intake overall. It's really quite remarkable.

WHM PROTOCOL: BASIC MINDSET EXERCISE

The greatest accomplishment you can achieve is stillness of the mind. It is only when your mind is still that you can go from external to internal programming. In the absence of thoughts, this stillness brings your feelings into alignment with your innermost being, reflecting the true self in a direct mirror. This is how I was able to set all of my records, and you can do it too.

First, take a step away and find a comfortable place to sit down. Then begin to follow the breath.

Deeply in, letting go.

Deeply in, letting go.

Peacefully following the breath.

Deeply in, letting go.

Deeply in, letting go.

A sense of calm will begin to settle over you, and it is in this moment that you can set your mind. Begin to scan your body while visualizing what it is you are going to do. Perhaps you want to stay longer in the cold shower or achieve a new personal record for push-ups. Maybe you want to hold a particularly challenging yoga pose or take a longer bike ride than you ever have before. Now is the time to scan your body and set your intention. Take your time with it. Tell your body what you expect it to do. Scan yourself for how you feel. You will be able to detect any misalignment of your intention and your body's feeling. Just remain calm, keep breathing, and wait for the moment in which there is a sense of trust, of centered energy, of alignment.

Give power to that feeling with your breath and then go and do what you intend to do. Success.

My experience on Everest proved instructive, as I ran the marathon there confronted not only by snow and freezing temperatures, but also on approximately half the oxygen that is available at sea level. In order to battle cold, you need combustion, which requires oxygen. But when oxygen is in short supply, in comes the mind. The mind is able to activate the right hormones to allow for increased oxygen absorption. That's what I did on Everest, and I employed the same technique that day outside the museum in New York. It comes down to verified confidence and trusting that when I see it in my mind, it is going to happen. I had applied the same mindset to hundreds of previous challenges, and I gained confidence from that. I accepted my journey and trusted what I saw. And being in alignment with the moment, with what was happening, helped activate my body. It was primed to respond, and

I knew that I was going to perform at my best. On top of that, by entering consciously into the stress of the cold and adapting to it, I've learned how to activate the brain stem, which is believed to govern our survival instinct, our fight-or-flight response, and our desire both for food and to procreate, all of which are closely tied to emotion.

Cold and heat work like emotions too. Emotion in the end is biological, a biological stress within, expressed through hormones. By going consciously into the cold, you learn to deal with the adrenaline and epinephrine, but also the dopamine, the serotonin, the cannabinoids, and the opioids that your body produces naturally as a response to this stress. I didn't know it at the time, but that's what I was doing outside the museum. Now I know why I had such control. Dr. Kamler, who was monitoring me the entire time, had never seen anything like it before, and he's the authority on surviving in extreme conditions. He wrote the book on it.

"Standard medical dogma states that once your core temperature falls below 90 degrees, you stop shivering—a process that generates heat," Dr. Kamler later wrote. "From that point on, if a source of external heat is not provided, your body temperature will continue to spiral downward, and you will eventually die of hypothermia. Wim has proven this wrong. His body temperature dropped to 88 degrees and then came back up to 94 without any external heat source. He has dramatically shown us that there is incredible power within the human body that modern medicine does not clearly understand."[4]

Later, after we celebrated, Dr. Kamler and I appeared at a conference in the museum to discuss what had happened out on the street and how I did it. Three hundred people were in attendance, and I got up on stage and told my story to an American audience, in English, for the first time. I talked about first going into the water at Beatrixpark and feeling this connection. I talked about learning to activate deeper parts of my brain and body in reaction to environmental stress and how to do so consciously. I was so excited to be there with Dr. Kamler on the stage! But as I spoke, I could see skepticism creeping across faces throughout the audience.

But then, suddenly, somebody came out with an infrared camera and connected it to the big screen behind us, so that the audience could see all the imaging. And they asked me, without warning, "Wim, do you think you could warm your hand up within a minute at will?" I didn't know if I could do it because I had never tried. So, I thought about it for a moment and said, "Well, I already set the world record today, and I'm feeling good. I will try!" I put my hand up in the air, and on the screen, the imaging showed blue, which indicated a normal temperature. But then I focused my energy within myself and toward my hand. Within a minute, I was able to raise the temperature by 12 degrees. You could see it on the monitor clear as day. Even I was shocked—absolutely shocked by this validation. The color had changed from blue to red. Three hundred people saw that I was able to increase the temperature in my hand by 12 degrees Fahrenheit at will, and after that, there were far fewer skeptics in the audience.

I say fewer because there were then, as there are now and as there have always been, people who simply refuse to believe what they see. They think it's a trick or an illusion or that I possess some sort of superhuman ability, that I am a genetic freak. But all I am doing is harnessing the tremendous power of the mind, which, again, is an innate capacity we all have within us. As I said before, I'm no superhero, and I'm not a guru either. Anything I can do, you can do too.

That was a great evening, and I met some wonderful people. It was a very emotional experience for me because it was clear that I had touched people. My own little world I had made for myself had collided with the larger world, the official world of scientists and doctors and reporters. It uplifted my soul. I went to bed that night feeling as if I had really turned a corner, and I had. But my adventure in America was only beginning.

Early the following morning, I boarded a train bound for Long Island with Professor William Bushell, a leading researcher into the health benefits of meditation and a Fulbright Scholar. Professor Bushell had spent nearly twenty years in the department of anthropology at MIT and also had academic affiliations with Harvard and Columbia Universities. We were headed to the Feinstein Institute for Medical Research in Manhasset to meet with the Institute's director, Dr. Kevin Tracey, and conduct some experiments. It was a pleasant, forty-minute ride, so Professor Bushell and I settled in and got to know each other. "Listen, what we can do is so much more than we think," I said. He had just published a major scientific work, entitled *Longevity, Regeneration, and Optimal Health* in conjunction with the New York Academy of Sciences, and after witnessing what I had done outside the museum and on its stage, he was very interested in hearing what I had to say. Professor Bushell is a kind man, extremely knowledgeable, and his support and friendship have helped boost our credibility in the scientific community immeasurably.

Dr. Tracey and his staff wanted to conduct an experiment on my vagus nerve, or the tenth cranial nerve, which is autonomous and for a long time has been believed to be beyond our will. Many experiments had been conducted on a wide range of test subjects over many years, and they had all shown that there was no way a human being could influence, consciously or otherwise, their vagus nerve. The vagus nerve relates very much to inflammation though, so if we were somehow able to influence it, we could potentially suppress inflammation and, by extension, treat and perhaps even reverse disease. How that could be done, however, was unknown. And that is why they brought me out to Manhasset.

They led me into a nice, comfortable room and asked me to have a seat. Then they inserted a needle in one of my arms to withdraw blood and connected my other arm to a heart-and-lung monitor. "Now meditate," they said. Once again, I didn't know exactly what I was supposed to do, but I resolved to just do my best. So I started to do my breathing exercises and learned, much to the consternation of the researchers, that when you do not breathe for two minutes straight, a heart and lung monitor will register a flatline, like you're dead. They didn't know that, though, and assumed instead that the monitor was malfunctioning. So I just went on with my breathing exercises while they went and got a new monitor and reconnected me. But a few minutes later, the same thing happened because I regularly go longer than two minutes without taking a breath when I do my breathing technique. So yes, there was another flatline, and the researchers were confused because they didn't know that I was causing it, and there was nothing at all wrong with the machine. So, what they decided to do when they hooked me up to the third machine was to withdraw blood simultaneously, which enabled them to get the data they needed. They told me it would take a week for the results because they'd be analyzing 307 different blood markers to see if I was influencing my vagus nerve.

While awaiting the results from the Feinstein Institute, I got on a plane and flew to Duluth, Minnesota, to visit the Hypothermia Lab at the University of Minnesota Medical School. Two world-renowned physiologists, Drs. Robert Pozos and Larry Wittmers, the lab's director, met me there and monitored my core body temperature and vital signs while immersing my body in ice-cold water for intervals of fifteen and then twenty minutes. The physiologists were both amazed that I was able to maintain my core temperature, as neither had ever seen anything like it before despite studying the cold for years. "The usual response to a shock or a cold was completely obliterated," Wittmers later told ABC News. "There was no—

Sitting in ice water at the University of Minnesota Medical School

none of the usual response you would see. And those responses that you see in most individuals that are exposed to that type of situation are uncontrollable."[5]

After that, we returned to New York, and soon after, I received a telephone call from Dr. Kamler. He had the results of the experiments at the Feinstein Institute, and he was really excited to share them. "If you are able to reproduce what you have done," he said, "it means huge consequences for humankind." Then he rattled off about twenty different conditions and diseases, from arthritis to Crohn's, that we could now battle because the control I had shown over my vagus nerve was unprecedented. The experiment showed that I was controlling an autonomous mechanism at will, which meant in turn that I was able to control inflammation, the cause and effect of so many diseases. The medical applications seemed, to Dr. Kamler, limitless.

What if we really are able to get the cause and effect of disease within the control of our mind? Wouldn't that be amazing? It happened in Manhasset. And as Dr. Kamler spoke, I was overcome by a tremendous sense of purpose, a direct knowing. *Yes,* I said to myself. *I can do this. I've awakened this state consciously, and I can show others how to do it too.* And there, at that moment, my true mission was born. I'm the missionary, remember? Remember how, at my birth, my mother had said, "Oh God, let this child live. I will make him a missionary"? Well it was at that exact moment, I realized that my mission is to bring this knowledge to humankind because everybody is able to do this. I was inspired and fully charged with my mission, and with that powerful realization, a sense of faith and destiny awakened to my being. It was transformative.

A half hour later, I received a telephone call from my wife. My mother had died. She had fallen, gone into a coma, and died. She had pledged to make me a missionary, and now, at the moment the mission had at last come into my vision, she was gone. It was as if she knew. I had a hole in my heart, but I was also filled with hope. I thought, *Mom, be in peace. You did so good. I will serve my mission and honor you by spreading my message to as many people as I can. I will return happiness, strength, and health back to where it belongs, Mom — to the soul, and to our consciousness, where life and love are fully blooming.*

In the weeks that followed, Dr. Kamler, Dr. Tracey, and I made plans by telephone to conduct a comparative study at a Buddhist retreat in the Catskills of New York. I was to train a group of test subjects to control their vagus nerve in the same way I had demonstrated I could. Only it never happened. Instead, suddenly there was radio silence from New York. I didn't understand. They had conducted study after study with others that failed to achieve the results we achieved, but for some reason there was no continuation of the research.

It was disappointing of course, but I was not overcome. I continued to walk the path of my mission. Three years later I made a connection with Vincent Wijers, director of the Circus of Thoughts, a show performed at the famed Royal Theater Carré in Amsterdam. He had heard about my story and had been inspired by my conviction. He wanted to put me on stage in the nearly two thousand–seat theater and pack me in ice for an hour or more to demonstrate that I was able to control my core body temperature. An experiment would occur ahead of time under the supervision of Professor Maria Hopman, a physiologist at Radboud University Medical Center in Nijmegen, and it would later be replicated onstage for Circus of Thoughts.

When I arrived at the theater, there were at least twenty people and even more monitors. They had prepared a bizarre experiment for me — eighty minutes in the ice with one arm removed so blood could be drawn. I swallowed a pill-sized device able to measure my core body temperature and display its readings on a remote monitor. They put a bunch of sensors on me to measure my skin temperature. They took thirty-six vials of blood over the eighty minutes and sent them to six different laboratories for analysis.

It was all very strange, like a scientific circus, and as a result, it attracted a lot of attention at the university. Many people came to see what all the commotion was about, including Dr. Mihai Netea, one of the Netherlands' greatest minds and one of the world's leading scientists studying the evolution of the human immune system. What Dr. Netea and his colleagues observed was incredible to them of course, and more than remarkable because they knew that physiologically what I was doing wasn't supposed to be possible. Yet there I was. During the entire eighty minutes in which I was exposed to the ice, my core body temperature remained at a constant 98.6 degrees Fahrenheit. My heart rate remained low, and my blood pressure remained within the normal range.[6]

Professor Hopman's study showed that my metabolic rate increased by 300 percent during the period of exposure, and this increased metabolic rate resulted in an increase in the heat production of my body. "Despite eighty minutes of full-body ice immersion and significant heat loss through the skin, [the subject's] core body temperature was maintained probably by an increased energy expenditure (and therefore heat production)," Dr. Hopman wrote in her case report. "This individual may have influenced the autonomic nervous system, thereby actively regulating the cardiovascular system and thermoregulation."[7]

The doctors were all astonished, but I knew what I — or rather what my mind — was capable of. I had also primed my biochemistry for performance by doing my breathing routine in the car on the way over to the university. My metabolic activity had increased to the point that I simply didn't feel the cold. So even though my skin temperature dropped to close to zero, it was like I had switched the heater on within my body. I felt great. I was able to function and to talk to everybody who came up to me and to answer their endless questions. I wasn't shivering or suffering at all. In fact, it was quite the opposite.

The doctors had taken a lot of my blood during the experiment, so they decided to conduct some experiments on it in addition to their analysis. And one thing they did was expose the samples to bacteria known to cause a violent reaction when exposed to immune cells. But in my blood, there was zero reaction. Seeing that and imagining the possible medical applications with regard to treating viruses and bacterial infections, Dr. Nitea asked me if I would be willing to participate in a further experiment. Together with Drs. Peter Pickkers and Matthijs Kox, Dr. Nitea proposed injecting me with an endotoxin — a bacteria — to see if and how my body's immune system would react.[8] They had injected this bacteria, *E. coli*, into more than 240 subjects previously, and every one of them had experienced flu-like symptoms, such as fever, chills, and headaches as a result. But because my blood had not reacted to the bacteria outside of my body, they were curious to see if my body could suppress the inflammatory markers commonly caused by the injection. I agreed.

A short while, after I returned to the university hospital, they took my vital signs and baseline measurements and then asked me to lie down on a bed. They connected me to all kinds of wires and monitors, and then Dr. Pickkers injected me with the bacteria, explaining that it would take sixty to ninety minutes to take effect. I began doing my basic breathing protocol preventatively, and an hour later, I didn't feel anything. No fever, no headache, no muscle aches. Nothing. I was just doing my breathing, and what the doctors observed on the monitors was that my blood-oxygen saturation levels, which at sea level should normally fall within the range of ninety-five to one hundred, had dipped all the way down to thirty. People normally die at fifty, mind you, but I was going deliberately to thirty, which caused the measurement device to shut off, as if I had died. Like the experiments at the Feinstein Institute, it was another flatline. But I was very much alive and feeling quite good. Deeply relaxed, actually. I had entered into a controlled hypoxic state, which can be very beneficial for the body. In fact, the Nobel Prize in physiology was recently awarded to three researchers whose work focuses on how cells adapt to changes in the level of oxygen, specifically the positive effect on cell metabolism and functions of the body overall when oxygen levels are low.[9]

The doctors withdrew blood every five or ten minutes and then sent it to the laboratory for measurement and analysis to determine whether or not the interleukin IL-6, IL-8, or IL-10 tumor necrosis factors were being affected. In layman's terms—and I am a layman—IL-6 and IL-8 are both pro-inflammatory proteins, and IL-10 is anti-inflammatory. Tumor necrosis factor refers to cell-signaling proteins that kill cancer cells. So the blood results showed that I was suppressing the inflammatory markers IL-6 and IL-8. This is significant because of the proliferation and outrageous cost of IL-6 inhibiting "biologic" injectable drugs that a growing number of people with autoimmune diseases, like multiple sclerosis and rheumatoid arthritis, now rely on.

I showed a direct suppression of the IL-6 without injecting anything. We announced the blood results on television, and I cried because I was so happy. Finally, all the suffering due to my true nature being suppressed, because of all the ridicule, lifted. I was able to share what I had learned about the power of the mind with the world, and I had the brain scans and blood samples to back it up. The evidence was compelling. The only problem was that scientific evidence is only valid if it's done with a comparative group. I was just N=1, and one test subject doesn't make scientific proof. For years I had been dismissed as a freak of nature, a genetic anomaly, a physiological marvel. Others derided me as a charlatan, a fake, a carnival attraction. *Come See the Amazing Iceman!*

We needed a test panel.

Dr. Pickkers's team asked me how many subjects and how much time I would need to spend with them. Six months? A year? I said, "Nah, ten days." And that became four days. In four days, I trained a panel of twelve male subjects to suppress the inflammatory markers in their blood. None of the twelve reacted to the endotoxin.[10] Not one became sick. The blood results showed that they were all suppressing the pro-inflammatory IL-6 and IL-8 markers while boosting their levels of IL-10. The tumor necrosis factor was on as well. It was incredible. We had done it! Finally, we had the proof we had been seeking. We were no longer a test panel of one.

I had taken these twelve men to my training camp in Poland, near the Czech border, to prepare them for the experiment. They weren't special or remarkable really, in any way, but they each gave me 100 percent of their focus. More than that, they gave me their trust. This is why, though I had originally estimated it would take ten days to complete their training, I decided to accelerate things by taking them up Mount Śnieżka—elevation 5,259 feet—on just the fourth day. I had only ever taken three others up there before, but I knew that going into wild nature has the power to bring you into a state of fear, of excitement. The mountain was unknown to them. They would have to hand themselves over to it just as they would have to do in the experiment. None of the group had any cold-weather mountaineering experience, it was negative 14 degrees Fahrenheit—which is *freezing cold*—and we were bare-chested in shorts. But we did our conscious breathing, went up the mountain, and twenty-five minutes later, we were all sweating. When we came to the ridge and looked over to the other side, we saw Czech military personnel all dressed up like ninjas. Just their eyes were uncovered. They saw us coming up and were so flabbergasted that they asked us to take selfies with them. That made the guys feel like badasses for sure. And from there, we decided to go for the summit, where it was negative 17 degrees Fahrenheit with extremely high winds. Mount Śnieżka is one of the windiest places in all of Europe, so it was really blowing, and the wind chill made it feel even colder. Naturally, when we reached the summit, we danced the Harlem Shake. We felt great! That's when I knew that the guys were ready. They were awakened and connected inside to a greater energy than they had previously known. And four days later, they were in the hospital being injected with an endotoxin that all but one of the 16,135 people participating in the study experienced an adverse reaction from. I was the only one who had managed to suppress a reaction previously. And when these twelve men also suppressed a reaction, it changed science. The study was published in both *Nature* and the *Proceedings of the National Academy of Sciences of the United States of America*, two of the most respected scientific journals in the world.[11] It was also adapted into a full chapter in the textbook *Biology Now*, so now it is being integrated into American science curriculums in both high schools and universities.[12]

But while the findings made the national TV news in the Netherlands and were subsequently published in those leading journals and textbooks, there was, much to my astonishment, little interest from the scientific establishment. After years of enduring the derision of skeptics, we showed definitively that a panel of twelve subjects, employing my method, had been able to tap into their autonomic nervous systems and not only successfully battle bacteria, which causes inflammation, but suppress it at will. The blood doesn't lie, and the results were there for anyone to see. All of that was previously unknown, unprecedented. I thought we deserved a Nobel Prize because we proved that we're able to address the cause and effect of disease. I thought we would inspire further experiments and investigations. But scientists can be a stubborn lot sometimes. They can move as slow as a turtle.

I was disappointed of course, but I'm not waiting for a Nobel Prize. I don't need that kind of external validation. If you engage too much in outside validation, you lose the path to yourself. You get off course. Self-love is being proud of yourself by your own lights. What is your best? Move toward that, not the best of your neighbors. Back yourself. Care for yourself. Not by protecting your ego, no, but by remaining present for your being when you feel most afraid, most uncomfortable, or awkward. Be calm in your love for yourself. It will enable you to see others more clearly and with more compassion. Don't seek to change others; change yourself. Just mind your own mind and let others mind theirs. Show them who you are through your actions, through your conviction. Be clear and transparent, vulnerable. If I cared what others thought of me, I would have stopped going a long time ago. I would have been eaten by the system.

I just keep on. This is my mission. I want to reveal the truth and to share it with the world. Not my personal truth or the kind of truth you find in textbooks, even *Biology Now*. No. I'm talking about the real truth of nature — the only truth — expressed through my belief and the love of my mother. Life is a mystery, and I embrace it. My heart is full. And my mind is certain.

In the winter, we host a series of week-long retreats in Poland. It's dark, gloomy, and bloody cold. But for many, it is one of the best experiences of their lives. When we go into the mountains, we say, "No ego, we go." We venture forth wearing nothing but shorts and shoes, bare-chested against the cold. We are one body. Becoming one with a group is so good for the individual. Together we go, and together we get back to Mother Nature. And when we reach the top of the mountain, where the winds whip our bodies mercilessly, nobody is talking anymore. Everyone is listening. Surviving. And what happens is that everyone begins to feel. Everyone is existing in an experience, at least for a moment, beyond the mind. Suddenly there is a stillness, a sensation that transcends these thought processes because the deeper parts of the brain are being revived and reset. I've experienced this sensation so many times now that the power for me is in the sharing. Sharing such natural wisdom with others is very exciting, a heightened state of awareness. Humans are tribal, and as such, communication with others creates solutions guided by feelings, but rooted in common sense.

When I have climbed Mt. Kilimanjaro with groups of people, we have pushed right up to the end, but that is not because I needed to boost my ego by reaching the "finish line," no. The finish line is illusory. It does not exist. But I make sure we meet our goals. Because in the end we are there to be pioneers, to create a new ground in the mind of society, new possibilities. And each person is united with their purpose. Step by step we go. I've been caught in whiteouts in the middle of Mount Everest. I've gone into the unknown in my shorts and lost my way. I've been under the ice and lost my way in the cold water. I've lost the way so much that it's where I discovered the true power of my mind. It's where I discovered my true resilience, how my mind was able to keep myself still and feeling good despite desperate, even dangerous circumstances. But I am not attached to achieving these things. I am not an idiot. If I feel it is dangerous, I will turn back—I have no problem with that. But I have learned that setting challenges for myself triggers deeper realities within me. Ultimately, the goal is to be more of myself. My ambition is always powered by my mission, my purpose. I set goals not to break them, necessarily, but to be in that moment when I am one with the reality of now, when the last step informs the next step, when I can only move through as I feel. It is amazing what purpose and conviction can do. Get your heart in it, into anything you do, and if you can't, then you seriously have to tune in and cleanse yourself to get back on track.

You don't need to venture beyond the Polar Circle or to the middle of the desert to experience this sensation, but you do need to venture beyond your comfort zone. The mind without thoughts is always still, always confident. Just follow the power of the mind, and you will get through the worst, most stressful situations. Cold, heat, and emotion are all stress. They're all biochemical in the end, or at least they translate that way. These methods enable us to deal with that stress and so much more armed with nothing more than the power of our minds. We go into the cold, we breathe, and we overcome stress while remaining in complete control over our happiness, strength, and health. Who doesn't want that?

The effectiveness of the method is no longer in question. It's proven. It has stood up to scientific scrutiny, and it's supported by scientific, nonspeculative data. It's up to you to take on the method and to be determined in doing it. You don't need to be a yogi for twenty years to get into those deep altered states of both your mind and your body. I'm a simple man, and I want to change the world. You see it, eh? You can see it because you know that change on this scale occurs not through the influence of money or the manipulation of power structures but by showing scientifically that we are more capable than we ever thought possible. We can alter the fate and destiny of our lives and return them back to the soul. This isn't some sort of abstraction; it's the power source of our happiness, strength, and health. It's driven by love, and that is what I wish to give to my children and all my beloveds, with respect to all living beings in nature and Mother Nature herself.

WHM MEDITATION

The origins of meditation date back to 5000–3500 BCE, yet it's constantly evolving. When you do the conscious breathing protocol, you are already doing a form of meditation, training your mind and connecting with your innermost depths. The principle of meditation is to follow something that does not excite the thinking brain. We take something very simple and follow it until deep peace comes over us. Here is one way to get acquainted with this peace.

1 Sit down in a safe, comfortable place and clear your mind.
2 Start connecting to your breath. Let yourself breathe naturally.
3 Start counting your breaths. Each inhale and exhale is one count. Count your breaths up to seven, and then from seven back to one. If you find yourself suddenly thinking about your daily life and your to-do list, return to counting the breaths. You will eventually find yourself able to just count the breaths, up to seven and back down again. The blood flow will go into the deeper areas of your brain, awakening feeling, not thoughts. Let the feeling become stronger. Follow the feeling and go as deep as you want. As you go along, the counting will fade away, like a song fading out. Follow the feeling and go deep into yourself, deep into peace.

1 While seated or lying down, take 30 to 40 full conscious breaths: Breathe fully in to the belly and the chest, then letting go, without force.

2 On your final exhale, let the air out and hold it out for as long as you can without discomfort. Listen to your body and don't force it!

3 When you feel the urge to breathe again, take a deep breath in, hold for 10 to 15 seconds. Then release and relax.

4 Repeat the steps above two or three more times, paying attention to how you feel and adjusting your breath as needed.

5 Rest in this elevated state until you are ready to move on with your day. Alternatively, use the energy you just generated for your morning workout or yoga practice. Experiment with what feels right for you.

Congratulations! You just influenced key drivers of your health, increased your vitality and focus, busted your stress, reduced inflammation factors, and optimized your immune system.

FOR COMPLETE WHM BREATHING INSTRUCTIONS AND SAFETY GUIDELINES, SEE **CHAPTER 4**.

Your post-breathing practice state is the perfect time to program your mindset. Try this:

1 Before you get up from your breathing practice, bring up a thought in your mind like "Today I'm going to stay in the cold shower for 15 more seconds than yesterday," or "I feel happy, healthy, and strong."

2 Reflect on this thought and notice how your body feels.

3 If you identify any inner resistance to your intention, just keep breathing steadily until you feel an alignment between your body and mind.

With practice, your sense of your inner experience, or interoception, will sharpen, allowing you to more consciously observe and control your body and mind.

SEE **CHAPTER 12** FOR DETAILS.

1 At the end of your warm shower, turn the water to cold.

2 If you like you can start by first putting your feet and legs, than your arms, then your full torso under the water.

3 Do NOT do the WHM Basic Breathing Exercise while standing in the shower.

4 Gradually extend your exposure every day until you can handle two minutes in the cold.

5 If you are shivering when you get out, try the horse stance exercise. (See page 118 for details.)

Success! You just improved your metabolic efficiency, regulated your hormones, further reduced inflammation, and are enjoying the endorphins and endocannabinoids released in response to the cold.

FOR FULL COLD EXPOSURE INSTRUCTIONS AND SAFETY GUIDELINES SEE **CHAPTER 3**.

6 OLAYA

To move forward, sometimes you have to go back. In this case, that means going back to my years as a squatter. That was a formative time in my life, and I look back on it with great fondness. I played a lot of guitar, did a lot of yoga, and of course, it was there that I first felt my attraction to the cold. I went into the water in Beatrixpark, and from there, I gained a new depth to my life, a new connection to nature and to my inner self that wasn't there before. I explored more and more, testing and experimenting, staying out in freezing temperatures all night long wearing nothing but shorts like some kind of lunatic.

I'm not into politics, I'm into freedom. And in the squatter's home, which was a large, abandoned orphanage, I was surrounded by free thinkers — poets, artists, and musicians — dwelling there with free minds, letting go. Letting go of judgment, of preconceived notions, allows you to see where you're really at, and that's what I was able to do in those years. To take stock of who I was and who I wanted to become. So many of us today are afraid or unwilling to let go. Our lives are governed by rules, morality, and a sense of ethics driven by conformity, and informed by the commotion of politics and the unceasing cycle of current events. This has caused us to become too narrow-minded in our perception of the world, which is the opposite of freedom.

I didn't know it at the time, but the freedom I enjoyed while living there is what allowed me to first see the path I have followed for the past forty years. It enabled me to get in contact with my own well-being. It inspired me to create, write poetry, and talk excitedly about all kinds of subjects, from philosophy to culture to the nature of existence, and to express my ideas freely and lovingly through art. Nobody was depressed or disillusioned. Nobody was stressed-out. And it was there, within the possibility of that freedom, that I first found and forged my connection with the cold water.

Seekers who are free within become finders. It's quite impossible to find anything meaningful when you are caught up in the stress of daily life, which can be all-consuming. Once you are able to detach from that stress, a new reality can enter your consciousness. The old orphanage was quite large, and it contained two interior courtyards. The courtyards offered a bit of seclusion but also an expanse of open sky. And in the wintertime, when it was cold and there was snow on the ground, I would sit naked all night long in one of the courtyards, practicing what would, in time, become my method. I could practice there anytime I wanted, naked as the day. There is nothing shameful about being naked, but hey, I didn't want to be disturbed, so I sat by myself. I remember sitting there and feeling such a power inside myself, like I was ruling over the elements of nature! It brought me into the depths of myself, though I didn't yet know how or why. All I knew is that it felt great and that I wanted to feel that way all the time.

One time I was doing yoga naked in the courtyard, and one of the women there thought it would be funny to put her feet near my genitals. But there was no arousal, no nothing. I was deeply into the yoga and had real control over myself. People were astonished, saying, "Hey, nothing's happening. What's the matter with you?" But nothing was the matter with me at all. I love women, and I've got six children to prove it. But I don't get aroused if I'm not into it, that's it. I have power over my own sexuality. I gained that power through exposure to the cold. The cold activates the adrenal axis in the brain stem, and the brain stem commands not only our fight-or-flight response, but our innate urge both to secure food and to procreate. They're all a part of our primordial survival instinct. Hardwired. But my experiences with the cold enabled me to gain control over those instincts and also the emotions that attach themselves to them.

Beatrixpark sat roughly a quarter mile from the squatter's home, and there I found my own space between two trees, two willows, so nobody could see me. I would go there every day, like a ritual, to charge myself up. Into the cold water but also into myself. My mind really set. Twenty-five deep breaths, a dynamic meditation. I would go to my spot between the two willows, and while undressing myself, I'd look out at the water and feel its presence. There it was. And then, once I entered the water, I'd charge myself up through the breathing, feeling at first a pleasant tingling sensation but then intensifying, as if my body was a beam of electricity. After the twenty-fifth breath, I'd submerge my entire body beneath the icy surface of the water, only keeping my hands on the edge of the hole for guidance. This is in no way part of my method because it is so dangerous. You could easily black out and drown. But that is what I was doing then.

Once I was beneath the ice, I would hear nothing at all. I would feel nothing but a deep sense of peace. It was like rebirth. I'd remain there beneath the ice at first for one minute, then two, three minutes, building up to four minutes without breath, and then beyond. After six or seven minutes, I would feel an urge to urinate, which was a signal to come back up toward the surface. And when the real need for breathing came, I'd just pull myself easily out of the water. Remaining in the mind, not cold or shivering at all, just being. Natural. I'd come out, get dressed, and do my exercises right there by the waterside, completely in control and within myself. And in that state, I was able to do somersaults, perform splits, do push-ups, whatever. It was like my body had gained an untold power. And the more I did it, the stronger this power became.

It was within my awakening to this power that I met the woman I would marry. I was at a gathering at the squatter's home and saw her dancing. She was so beautiful. Long curly hair, bright eyes, full lips, just lovely. There she was dancing right in front of me, and

I was mesmerized. Just absolutely transfixed. And then, to my aston-ishment, she came over and sat down next to me. She told me her name, Olaya. So beautiful. We were talking and laughing, and it all felt so easy, so natural. Then the group we were with decided to go for a walk, to Vondelpark, and I was glancing over at her the whole time. But it wasn't just me. She was glancing back. Something was happen-ing there — there was an energy between us — but then, suddenly, she was gone. I had gone for a quick dip in the pond there in Vondelpark, and she disappeared. I was heartbroken. So I went and sat down on the stage where they do performances in the park, and then, from out of nowhere, I felt hands on my back. It was Olaya, and she was giving me a massage! And in that moment, I truly let go. No fear, no inhibition. I just grabbed her and hugged her, and I knew right then and there that we were in love. We joined hands and danced all the way back through the city to the squatter's home as if on a cloud.

We slept together that night, but we did not have sex. We just slept together with our clothes on and embarked upon a platonic yet very sensitive relationship, very emotional, very much present. It may seem odd, but it went on that way for about a year. There was no need for sex because we were connecting on a different level. The connection was so strong, it was clear that nothing more was needed. We just loved each other, and when we were together, it was as if we existed outside the bounds of time. It was, instead, like living in the pure emotion of the moment. That's how I remember it, at least. And it was beautiful.

After about a year, she had to return to Spain, to Basque country. She was gone for about five months, and I grew lonely without her. Then one day a letter arrived. She was coming back to Amsterdam in one month, and of course I was waiting. When she returned, so did the energy between us, and this time the energy manifested itself physically. We became lovers. But then, after four months, she went away again, back home to Spain, and I thought it was over.

Olaya remained on my mind and in my heart of course. A force like hers isn't soon forgotten, and it took about four or five months for that emotion within me to still. I was missing her so much that it was interfering with who I was and what I was doing, but in time I was finally able to regain control over my emotional state. But soon another letter arrived, and this time it said that she was nearly six months pregnant. So I did what anyone in my situation would do. I went immediately to the rail station and boarded a train headed for Paris. And from Paris to Pamplona. In those days, there weren't any mobile phones, and she had left me no phone number to call. All I had was the letter. But I was on my way, straight as an arrow; I was going to be a father, and my heart swelled with pride.

I arrived in Pamplona and was received by Olaya's family. Her father had these intense blue eyes, and he set them upon me in a way nobody ever had before. They pierced straight into me, penetrating my being as if he were trying to examine my soul. I met his stare with eyes that said, *I'm here to own up to my responsibilities as a father. I love your daughter deeply, and I will do whatever it is I have to do to take care of her and our child.* After that his gaze softened, and I was accepted by the family. They knew my intentions were honorable.

I'm an identical twin, as you know, but so was Olaya. She had a sister named Siuri. I remember walking around Pamplona, in the natural beauty of Basque country, just proud to be following these extraordinary women. They were talking to each other, and I was following the drift of it all as best I could since my Spanish was not so great. Sometimes I couldn't follow the conversation, but I was there, and my heart was there, and love is a universal language. She had waited more than five months to tell me that she was pregnant! But after two weeks in Pamplona, we both knew what we had to do. And we returned to Amsterdam together.

I had no money of course, and I was still living in the squatter's home. But we had love and respect for each other, and we found a way through. When it came time for Olaya to deliver the baby, we had to call a cab. And I was so poor that I could hardly afford the cab fare to the hospital. Fortunately for us, health care in the Netherlands is universal, so we didn't have to worry about the cost of a hospital stay.

We arrived at the hospital around 10:00 p.m., and at 5:00 a.m. sharp, our son Enahm was born. It was March 22, 1983, but I remember it like it was yesterday. He had ten fingers, ten toes, and all the love in the world. After another day or two, we went home, settled in, and there we were. A family.

There is a law in the Netherlands that requires parents to register the name of a child within three days of their birth, so I had to go down to the municipality to register him. The only problem was that I had no name, so the name I gave him is "a name." In Dutch, "a name" is *een naam* but they didn't understand that because I spelled it a bit differently, putting an *H* just before the *M*. Enahm. Everyone said, "Wow, what a beautiful name," which made me laugh. I only called him "a name" because I had no other name for him. Thirty-seven years later, my son is still called "A Name," and many people still ask, "Where does that name come from? It's an exotic name, a strange name." And I don't want to disappoint them, so I usually play along. But back then I had no name, and now he has A Name (Enahm)! That's it!

Enahm was a happy baby, very agreeable, laughing all the time. You know what I did with him? From a tender age, I began taking him into the cold water. Just a quick dip—no ice swimming! He would gasp at first, startled, and then he would laugh and laugh. He emanated so much energy for such a little thing. We did this on a regular basis, and he loved it. And I think this contributed to him being a very healthy, strong baby, laughing all the time, rarely sick. We had a great time with him. We didn't worry about this or that as many new parents do. We were not inhibited in any way in our love for him. And when you have a great time with your baby and the baby is growing nicely, growing strong and happy, the idea of a second baby—and a third and a fourth—makes sense. Even when you have no money. So that's what we did.

We named the second baby, a daughter, Isabelle. Isa for short. She was a truly beautiful baby, with the most beautiful blue eyes I had ever seen. She's thirty-five years old now, and she works with me, together with her brother Enahm, and yes, her sister, Laura, and brother Michael, who came soon after. Laura had the biggest eyes you could ever imagine on a baby, and we named Michael after Michael Jackson, the American pop star. I loved Michael Jackson's music back then, and I still do.

After Isa was born, we knew we had to leave the squatter's home. Suddenly I was thrust back into the system I had rejected eight years prior, and my reentry into that world, with its rules and conventions, was difficult. I was confronted by all this square thinking, people complaining that our children made too much noise. To me they seemed oversensitive, incapable of accepting life as it is, living narrow-mindedly. That kind of living makes people stressed, and then, when little children play — *as children do* — it becomes a disturbance. I had to go to court at one point because the other tenants in the building where we lived wanted us out. The children were making too much noise, they said. The whole thing was ridiculous, but it made it clear to me that we needed to make a change.

We packed up the children and the few things we had, and we went to Spain, into the mountains. My brother Rudie drove us. We found a place in Iturgoyen, about twenty-five miles from Pamplona. It was a big, old house. Nobody had lived there for ten or fifteen years, and suddenly it was ours. A rental. I had to find work of course. So I went to the village and found a job posting for an English teacher. A school in Estella, about nine miles to the south, needed somebody who could speak both Spanish and English. I wasn't exactly fluent in either language then, but I figured I knew enough to get by. So I filled out an application and was fortunate to get hired. I also began to learn to speak Basque, which is a completely different language from Spanish, but very beautiful. Learning how to speak Basque enabled me to better communicate with Olaya, her family, and the people both in Iturgoyen and the surrounding area.

The Basque people have cultural and political differences with the Spanish government, and they have been repressed for a long time. The Spanish want everything to be Spanish and for Spanish culture to be the dominant culture of the region, but the Basque are a proud people with a rich tradition. Spain at the time was still recovering from Franco's fascist regime, which had made a lasting imprint on the culture. There was also the Euskadi Ta Askatasuna, or ETA, which was a Basque separatist organization and labeled a terrorist group by Spain, France, the UK, the United States, Canada, and the European Union following the ETA's violent campaign of bombings, assassinations, and kidnappings.[1] The ETA believed they were fighting for their cultural liberty and freedom, but their methods were extreme. I'm all for freedom, as I have made clear, but I'm not into killing. When it comes to fomenting change, I lean toward the Gandhi mold of nonviolence: there is no road toward peace; peace is the road. That's a philosophy I can get behind.

In the middle of all this political conflict, I remember one night sleeping at Olaya's parents' house in Pamplona, on the eighth floor, and dreaming. I dreamed that something terrible had happened, and boom, I woke up. "What happened?" I looked out the window and saw that there had been a car-bomb attack in the street below; three people were blown to smithereens. Three hours later, when I went down to the street, the Red Cross was still out there. I wasn't aware of what they were doing at first, but then I saw them gathering what looked like little pieces of meat, like bacon, from out of the shrubs and other vegetation lining the street. It was a sickening sight that I will never be able to forget.

With the specter of violence hanging over us, my wife, four children, and I encountered some difficult times. Not only did I have little money, but Olaya's mental state began to deteriorate. The darkness, the shadow, had begun to take shape and was gaining momentum. She had always been so open, extroverted, always talking, an absolutely unique being. It's very difficult to see someone you love dwelling in darkness and sinking deeper and deeper into it. We had found a great place in the mountains, away from the tumult of the city, and her family was nearby. My job was bringing in some money, albeit not enough. But the shadow grew and grew, and we couldn't stay any longer because she wasn't taking care of the children, and I wasn't able to do it by myself. So I took Olaya to her parents' home in Pamplona and took our children back to the Netherlands.

I had no house, no money, no job, and four hungry children to feed and clothe. Fortunately for me, the Dutch government offers generous social assistance benefits, and after a short investigation, they gave me a house to rent and a monthly payment—similar to welfare benefits in the United States—and I was able to sustain our life. But my Olaya was not there. When she would visit from Spain, I never knew which Olaya I would get. One day she'd be a great mother, and everything would be wonderful, but on other days, she would stay in bed and refuse to engage. She was depressed, very depressed, and it was only getting worse. With four children aged one to eight to care for, it was difficult for me to find (or even look for) work. And in society, if you have no money, no means, you have no value. But I did what I had to do to stay strong for my children. I practiced my yoga, took my cold baths, did my breathing, my postures, and kept believing that a brighter future was ahead of us.

That was a heavy period for sure, but I did not despair. The breathing and the cold really helped me deal with the stress, allowed me to let go, and at least in my mind, be free. My method became a practice and then a ritual as I struggled to find a place for myself and my family within a society that was largely insensitive to our plight. The children and I loved Olaya deeply, but we could no longer rely on her. She'd be gone for months at a time, so we learned instead to depend on ourselves and on each other. The older children had to grow up faster than I would have liked.

Things changed when Javier, a friend I had made in the Basque country, offered me a job leading organized trips for tourists in the Spanish Pyrenees. I had gone into the mountains with Javier before, back before canyoneering (or *barranquismo* as they call it in Spanish) was the sport it is now. The canyons were not equipped for exploration in those days, but we explored them anyway and saw spectacular things. The canyons are like live museums, prehistoric museums. There are strange monoliths everywhere, rocks and abysses. There is no time there. No ideas. Instead there's just this magnificent, quiet energy—an intense quiet—that left a mystical impression on me. I knew from those experiences that others would enjoy exploring the canyons, so I took a chance and accepted the job with Javier.

Between trips into the canyons, I had to find different ways to make money, so I took on work as a gardener. The work suited me, and I enjoyed it, but soon I turned my attention to a burgeoning side business. I taught kids how to climb trees in the garden safely and soon gained a reputation around Amsterdam for my tree-climbing birthday parties. The kids loved it. They wanted to climb! They wanted to feel what there is to feel beyond their fear, how to enjoy themselves freely, and find peace. That's what I saw in their eyes after these climbing sessions. They'd be sitting serenely in a circle eating brown bread or whatever there was, and their minds were still. Every last one of them.

Our children need to climb trees now more than ever. They need to do their Tarzan thing. The tree, too, is a teacher. It teaches the climber how to overcome fear, master their motor skills, and forge a mind-body connection. It's instant learning. Something they can't get from any video game. The kids don't know what it is; they just feel it. And they love how it feels. A tree is alive, and if a kid is in a tree when there's wind, he or she is alive with that tree going back and forth. They feel a deep connection, a kinship. It's strong. They've got to take care and be very cautious, and that brings them into the depth of their brain and body. They become very sensitive, alert, attuned to their surroundings.

That's what children want, no? Isn't that what we *all* want? Kids want to live wholly, experience everything. They want to be led by curiosity and love instead of fear. Kids know that feeling is knowing, so let the children play and leave them be.

The schools are teaching our children history, mathematics, and language, but it's time for children to also learn about cultivating happiness, strength, and health. Too many of them will grow up and go immediately into unsatisfactory careers, into stress. They will burn out. Many will develop autoimmune diseases, and it's all because they're stressing out too much. Over what? It doesn't have to be that way. Nature is within us, and it is within our children. Happiness, strength, and health — that's ours.

Play is a key. I'm a very playful person, and I loved to play with my children. I think sometimes I loved playing with them more than they did, you know what I mean? But I was just trying to do what I could to make them happy. It was just me and the four of them all alone. Their mother's shadow grew and grew. At this time, I started a canyoneering venture with Javier. It wasn't a big operation, but it was enough to sustain myself, to pay the bills. The method was coalescing. Bringing people through the canyons and into the mountains, where there was often cold water, helped bring things together. I was doing great with my breathing. I had rediscovered the spark of life, but the Olaya I knew was gone.

Further and further down she spiraled. Pills and injections, therapy, none of them could stem her descent into darkness. I tried my best to be there for her because she was the mother of my children, the love of my life. I still loved her madly, but there was little I could do. She was terrorized by her own mind. I needed to be strong for our children, to maintain as stable an environment for them as I could.

Olaya

And I did. We actually had a good time. We had our little nest, and we filled it with love.

In the summer of 1995, we went back to Spain because I was leading trips into the canyons, and it made sense to have the children nearby, where they could be looked after by Olaya's family. I remember, on the road to Spain, we were sleeping out under the stars, and she came to me. She wanted to make love and make another baby, but I said, "First, heal." We went to Spain, where we were received by her family, and I went off into the mountains. Three weeks later, I was on the job when I got a telephone call from Olaya's brother telling me that she had jumped from the eighth story, having kissed our children goodbye moments before.

I went directly back to Pamplona, and her father took me to see her. I saw her face, and it had been liberated of its shadow. The darkness had lifted. The demon, the terror was gone. Whatever it was that had split within her brain was gone. She had achieved peace and despite my heartbreak, in a way so did I. I felt her presence from up in the ethereal hemisphere and knew that she could see that I was doing well with our children. The love and emotion were still there — they still are to this day — well preserved, strong, and alive. New trees would grow and flourish from where she had gone. Those trees would bear fruit, and that fruit would nourish our souls.

Olaya's father and I cried together. We buried her soon after, and then I went back to the mountains to continue my job because I had to provide for my children. There was no time to mourn properly, to process the grief. Instead I sought peace in the canyons and within myself. This is how I sought to survive the grief of my broken heart. By getting back into the business of life. You can't dwell. If you've got four children, you just have to be there, you've got to be present, and you've got to press on.

Do you know what healed me? The cold water. It brought me back into reality. Instead of being guided by my broken emotions toward stress and sorrow, the cold water led me to stillness. Stillness of the mind. That gave my broken heart a chance to rest, restore, rehabilitate. And that's the way it went. The children made me survive, and the cold water healed me. Or maybe it was the other way around. Maybe the cold water made me survive, and my children gave me the strength to heal myself. They gave me a purpose to live and to be present for them 100 percent. When you go into the cold water, you're no longer thinking about your mortgage, your next meal, your emotional baggage. You're not caught up in your thoughts. It's freezing, and you're just surviving. That brought me to a place where I could heal. I loved my children deeply, and they were my salvation.

It was then that I first understood the true benefits of the cold water, breathing techniques, and positive mindset I was employing. So I made a method out of them, in the hope that others could benefit from them as I had. The breathing exercises are really simple and very effective. It only takes a few minutes to feel their power. I was priming and changing my biochemistry in the depths of myself, and I felt cleansed every time I did the breathing exercises. They quieted my mind and filled me with energy. They took me from acidic to alkaline and brought my body into a chemical environment within which I could go consciously into the mind, just as nature intended. Simple and effective. That was twenty-five years ago, and the method has evolved a lot since then, but its original spark is still with me. Like the memory of my dear, sweet love, Olaya, I carry it with me wherever I go.

7 WHM FOR HEALTH

Back in 2018 I trained a group of US Navy SEALs over a couple of days at the naval base in Pearl Harbor, Hawaii. On the first day, we worked on going into the cold, how to deal with stress and sleep deprivation, and how to control stress hormones in general. The SEALs, of course, are an elite military unit, and those guys already have all the techniques for surviving and thriving in adverse conditions down pat, but because they're also frequently sleep deprived and under tremendous amounts of stress, that's what I focused on. I wanted to help them get into their own bodies, get into their functionality, and ultimately, give them more control over their physical well-being, which would help them continue to perform at a high level no matter the circumstances.

Going into ice-cold water is very stressful on the body of course, but learning how to do it progressively, changing your biochemistry through breathing exercises, helps you to adapt quickly and to lessen the impact of that stress. Furthermore, it enables you to respond to the cold in a proactive way, not reactively. This is what I teach, and though these SEALs spend a great deal of time in the water and have a reputation for being arguably the toughest, most indefatigable fighting force in the world, many of them came to me to be taught. I thought that was amazing, and I was honored that they had placed their faith in me and my method. But when I arrived at the base on the second day, I wasn't sure what else it was that I could teach them. We'd pretty much covered it all on the first day I thought, and these men had little time to waste.

Just before reaching the checkpoint, coming into the base, I looked down at my phone and saw that I had received an email from a doctor, a general practitioner. Let's call her Jenny. She wrote:

> Dear Wim,
> Last year I jumped from a third-story window because I had had it with the pain. I woke up in the hospital, and my brother was there. When we were talking, he told me about you. I began to do what you are teaching, this breathing and this cold, and all. And now I'm thankful for every day that I'm alive.
> I love you,
> GP Jenny

It was in that moment that I realized what it was I had to offer the SEALs on the second day of training. Something always comes up from the moment. I don't go into these things prepared. I meet the moment. It informs me better. So I gathered all the men under the shade of a large tree, and I said, "Guys, today you are going to learn how to become the general within yourself and to stop the war within. Therein lie the real terrorists, in your mind, in your body. Let me show you how." We began to do the breathing, and they went very deep within themselves and found a peace that they had never before felt. Complete engagement with their breathing allowed them to become more aware of themselves, and in this moment their mission, their duty, fell away from their immediate consciousness. They were able to take a break from the pressures of life as a SEAL and exist within the stillness of an overwhelming calm.

"What do you think of life?" I said. "What is your destiny?"

"I just want to protect my family, my babies, my loves," one called out.

"Yes, that's it," I said. "That's the energy we bring into the world. When we tackle the real terrorist—disease, physical and mental—we can guarantee happiness, strength, and health for ourselves and those we love. If you are in tune, mentally and physically, with your true nature and sit within your heart, you become aware of the peace, happiness, and purpose that brings, you will be able to perform at your best." Their hearts were opened. The war was won.

I am privileged to meet many people from all over the world and from all walks of life through my mission; it has become an amazing movement. But the mission is still on—we have to fundamentally change our way of thinking. Now that more and more scientists have come to endorse and extol the method's benefits, I'm being met by less skepticism than I have in the past (though naturally some are still reluctant to embrace it). Many people who believe that they have been failed by doctors and pharmaceuticals are practicing the method and finding that they don't need medication anymore because they have instead unlocked their own innate capacity to deal with stress and that which causes it, whether it be a bacteria, a virus, or just the day-to-day anxiety inherent in navigating one's way through a complicated world and managing one's emotions, the volatility and uncertainty of it all. By now you should have a pretty good idea of how it is that they do it and how transformative the method truly is. If you follow these techniques as they have, if you breathe and go into the cold and, perhaps most importantly, have confidence in your own capacities, you too can move beyond the way we have been conditioned to think and behave and achieve true strength, health, and happiness.

We are not born half, we are born whole, and the way back into that is through the life-force. Can it really be so simple? Just breathing deeply? Is that it? The answer, friends, is yes. You've been breathing since the moment of your birth, but with what intention? With what purpose? When we change the paradigm and truly embrace the breath as *inspiration*, as dictionaries seek to define it, then we open ourselves up to the possibility of change. It's as simple as that. It's like I said at the outset: the breath is a door.

Many people who suffer from autoimmune conditions and other debilitating ailments and diseases have benefited greatly from the method. Crohn's disease is a terrible disease that often results in the surgical removal of intestines, colostomy, and endless medication, including, more often than not, harmful steroids.[1] The medical establishment, in all their wisdom, has developed no effective alternate remedies for Crohn's beyond pharmacological solutions and, to a degree, the careful management of a patient's diet. But practitioners of the method have found that when they begin to breathe, it reduces the inflammation associated with the disease and, with it, the need for medication. This is not an exaggeration. Reducing inflammation in the body is as simple as breathing. It's within your innate capacity as a human being and doesn't cost a dime. And its benefits aren't limited only to Crohn's sufferers.

WHM AND ULCERATIVE COLITIS

One of the most powerful moments in my life has been the discovery of the Wim Hof Method. Not only has it helped completely heal my autoimmune disease, but it has also given me a sense of purpose and contribution in helping thousands of others regain control over and reshape their lives in strength, health, and meaning. Back in 2006, I had been feeling depressed and stuck in my life, and not taking care of my health and diet as a result. I was going nowhere fast, and I was at a real low. My colon was seriously inflamed, and I was in a lot of pain. I was experiencing long hours on the toilet passing blood, and I had extremely low energy.

I was then diagnosed with ulcerative colitis, an autoimmune disease also known as IBD (inflammatory bowel disease), similar to Crohn's disease, and doctors told me I'd have it for the rest of my life.

For years I experimented with diet and nutrition, sport and exercise, yoga and meditation. I reshaped my life and routines, cut out damaging habits and activities, and although I was in remission (symptom-free) and medication-free for over five years, there were still limits to what I could eat, drink, and do. I still had to function within boundaries and be very careful . . . until I discovered the Wim Hof Method.

By following Wim's ten-week online course, I found a way back into my body and some deep healing took place over a matter of weeks. I felt renewed, and as a result, I now have no symptoms of my ulcerative colitis whatsoever. It's gone. The method allowed me to push way past my boundaries and define new ones. I now eat and drink with complete freedom and enjoy fitness and sports once more. I live a life of freedom that enables me to travel and work and live my dream of impacting others as a certified instructor of the method. I've never been stronger, healthier, or happier. And I'm never, ever sick.

RICHARD AYLING
BALI, INDONESIA

According to the Centers for Disease Control (CDC), 23 percent of American adults — more than fifty-four million people — have been diagnosed by a doctor with arthritis, a disease characterized by joint pain. Another forty million or so have reported symptoms consistent with an arthritis diagnosis. Among the fifty-four million who have been diagnosed, approximately twenty-four million report being limited in their activities as a result of their arthritis. That's a lot of suffering.[2] But it doesn't have to be that way.

While physical therapy, massage, and acupuncture (in addition to medication) have all helped arthritis sufferers alleviate their pain and discomfort to various degrees, the disease is not believed to be curable. But like Crohn's, it's a disease that's exacerbated by inflammation.[3] This is why so many people with arthritis take anti-inflammatory medications and, in severe cases, steroids. But what if you could drastically reduce the inflammation in your joints without taking any medication at all? What if you could get back to enjoying the physical activities you love without having to endure the pain and discomfort you have come to associate with them?

Henk van den Bergh is a Dutch blacksmith who lost his mother at the age of fifty-six due to complications stemming from rheumatoid arthritis. Nearing fifty himself, he came to me because his own rheumatoid arthritis had become severely debilitating. He could hardly work in the forge, and he was facing the likelihood of wrist and elbow surgery. He was in a lot of pain, and he was desperate. The medications his rheumatologist had prescribed weren't working, and he'd reached the point where he could barely walk. A friend said to him, "Go see Wim Hof," and figuring he had nothing to lose, he did.

Henk was one of about forty people who registered for one of my two-day workshops. It was held just a couple of towns over from where he lived, in Blaricum. At dinner on the first night, I sat across the table from him and got to know his story. He told me that he hated the cold and that his body was in such bad shape that he couldn't even ride his motorcycle anymore. He doubted that he could do a single push-up, let alone twenty, and he was thinking of quitting his job even though his business, the van den Bergh family forge, dated back to the 1830s.

"Tomorrow you're going to do forty push-ups," I said.

"Are you crazy?" he said.

"Yeah, sort of," I said. "But about life, you know." I looked him dead in the eyes. "Tomorrow you're going to do forty push-ups," I repeated, and he could tell that I meant it.

The next morning after breakfast, I took Henk aside and walked him through the breathing. He was skeptical and reluctant, but sensing my conviction, I suppose, he went along with it. People started to gather around us, and Henk realized that he'd reached a point where he couldn't turn back. He was convinced that it was madness, pure madness, but he resolved to try his best. He gave himself over to the breathing — fully and letting go, fully and letting go — thirty, forty times.

"And now, fully in," I said as I demonstrated. "Fully out. The last one: fully in, halt, and now go! Do push-ups!"

That's when Henk van den Bergh, a man who was so crippled by arthritis that he could barely walk, dropped down to the floor and banged out forty push-ups like it was nothing. Forty push-ups, can you imagine? The look on his face — his utter astonishment — I will never forget. It was as if the man had seen the face of God. Years of well-meaning doctors and medications had led him on a downward spiral in which he was now contemplating leaving behind the only life he ever knew, and here he was doing forty pain-free push-ups after only twenty or thirty minutes of breathing.

It was like a fucking miracle, you know? He was flabbergasted, just sitting there. Later we all went for an ice bath, and when it was his turn, he went in without hesitation.

And now, every morning during the winter, he takes a dip in the cold waters of a local lake, Gooimeer, with about sixty other towns-people. Henk has convinced them of the cold water's healing powers, and of course, he's a testament to it. He is now known locally not only for his stewardship of his family forge, which he has returned to full time, but for taking people into the cold. He's established a tradition of taking four or five hundred people into the cold water at the beginning of the year, something akin to the Polar Bear Plunge events that are used as charity vehicles in the United States. And his rheumatoid arthritis? Despite the irreversible damage to his joints, it's virtually gone. So thoroughly rehabilitated is Henk that in 2014, he participated in our expedition up Mount Kilimanjaro, the highest peak on the African continent. Amazing.

Henk isn't the only one who has been able to alleviate the symptoms of illness or eliminate diseases altogether by practicing the method. Far from it. There are, literally, thousands of others suffering from a range of medical conditions, from diabetes to Parkinson's, who have reaped great benefit to their health by breathing and taking on the cold. We've received thousands of testimonials, some of which we have included in this book, from people who credit the Wim Hof Method with helping manage and in a lot of cases eradicate the debilitating symptoms of various diseases and gain a new lease on life. It's remarkable and inspiring.

It is important for people, especially those suffering from such destructive diseases where they feel their own body has turned against them, to confront pain consciously. Getting into the cold water allows them to find themselves as the captain again — opening to the pain, welcoming it, reframing what it is to have pain, choosing change, not being a victim anymore. How do you think Henk felt when he did those push-ups? That first moment, when he realized what he just did, changed the story of himself. In that moment he had a future. This is not sorcery, or some guru telling you to do some crazy shit. You, in an instant, become your own inspiration. You feed off of your own new-found capability.

Well, how about we take that a step further? In the current way of thinking, we see "the pill" as the thing that is going to fix us. The method brings people back to their accountability, their self-awareness, often leading to a thorough change in lifestyle where they take things into their own hands. We may all want a paradigm shift in our culture, but you are the one with the responsibility to make it. Commit to it, dedicate yourself to it, especially if you have a severe condition. I have met many people who have avoided costly hospital stays because they have got their condition to a point where they can turn it around. If we can get people to take this up, we would need a lot fewer hospitals. Some of those buildings could instead be used as housing for the homeless or as public libraries that enable communities to deepen and enrich their knowledge instead of further perpetuating an on-going cycle of illness, surgery, and dependence on pharmacological solutions.

We acknowledge that we're not doctors, and we're not suggesting that the method can or should replace them. Medicine is still a noble profession, and I do believe that the majority of doctors enter the profession out of a duty to help people. But every day I'm hearing stories of people who defied their diagnosis and their doctor's orders and instead found relief from a whole host of symptoms, conditions, and diseases, from asthma to depression, MS to cancer, as a result of practicing the method. And that alone merits further investigation. The method is so effective, natural, and accessible that the general lack of interest shown by the medical establishment is quite puzzling to me. I'm no conspiracy theorist, and I want to believe that everyone involved has the best intentions, but perhaps the reason why some have dismissed me is that the method poses a threat to the existing order. Placing health back into the hands of patients and out of the hands of pharmaceutical conglomerates is, in a way, a revolutionary act. But there has got to be a better way, and I believe in my heart that

I have found it. This shit works, guys. It's real. So many people have been helped that it's become too much for me. I can't count that high.

The paradigm is shifting toward a more holistic, natural approach to health care, and the workshops we conduct are attracting a lot of people, so slowly but surely, we are getting through to the people who are ready to listen. It fills me with such gratitude. Five hundred people in Amsterdam, four hundred people in Barcelona. Large crowds in Munich, Poland, Melbourne, Sydney, Los Angeles. I'm going everywhere and spreading the news now, and everywhere I go, I hear new stories of how the method has helped people with their health. Even my gardener, the man who takes care of the WHM Center when I'm not here — and I'm not here a lot because I'm traveling so much — has found relief in the method. I love to tend my garden, but I can't do it all the time, so I hired Bertwin Hooijer to take care of it for me. Bertwin came to me suffering from depression and severe backaches that kept him up at night. But after immersing himself in the method, his depression and his backaches are both gone. In addition to his work in the garden, he helps me with the two-day retreats we conduct here locally, taking care of the ice baths and the fires, anything that comes up. People come from all over the world to attend these retreats, and Bertwin sees these people change their lives in profound ways, leaving here much happier than they had been just two days prior. That kind of happiness is infectious.

Stroe, where I live right now, is the most Catholic, and Christian in general, part of the Netherlands, but I'm not dealing with God here; I'm dealing with the divinity each and every one of us carries within. Not the kind with priests and yogis and churches though. No. You are your own temple, your own mosque, your own synagogue. So you've got to treat it well, be well therein, and make sure that you are in command because you want to feel great, you want to feel divine. Who doesn't? That's what I told Bertwin, and he really took it to heart. He's helping people get the benefits of the method now, paying it forward, as they say. He's still hoping to help his neighbor, who is relying on medication with his severe arthritis and who resists getting into the cold. But those biological drugs are expensive, man — nearly $3,000 a month for one injection. It's a big industry. And it's all based on the IL-6 interleukin, which, as we discussed back in chapter 5, is an inflammatory protein that we showed an ability to suppress during our experiments with Drs. Pickkers and Kox at Radboud.

A Polish doctor recently came to our Masters Module as part of our instructor training. He had hoped upon his return to Poland to convince his professor to conduct a study. If this goes through, there will be sixty subjects split into four groups of fifteen. One group will be the control group, one group will do the cold exposure, one group will do the breathing alone, and one group will do the breathing and the cold together. If the study or another like it is completed, we will see whether it supports the idea that the method effectively suppresses the IL-6 inflammatory marker.

Imagine what kind of impact this might have on the pharmaceutical industry and, hand-in-hand with them, the insurance companies. There are millions of people suffering from autoimmune diseases in the Netherlands alone, where the total population is only seventeen million people. How many might there be then in Germany, where the population is nearly five times that number, or in Europe as a whole? In America, the National Institutes of Health (NIH) estimate that up to 23.5 million people suffer from autoimmune diseases, and there's reason to believe that figure is low.[4] And if practicing the method truly can help people with autoimmune diseases suppress the IL-6 protein naturally, without the need for pharmaceutical drugs and no longer having to pay $3,000 a month, we're looking at trillions of dollars over the world. Trillions. The savings would be nearly $800 million annually in the United States alone.

Just think about what could be done with that money if it were reinvested in just causes and how many people we could help. These diseases are modern diseases, Western diseases, that are linked to stress caused by environmental factors, but we don't have to accept them. We don't have to bankrupt ourselves to pay for medicine that we don't need. Hell, my gardener is healing people now, man. His neighbor had severe arthritis, and now he is taking almost no medicine anymore. He has no pain. But many others are still suffering needlessly.

I'm a man of feeling, of enthusiasm. Every day offers a chance to tackle the problems of the world, of my beloveds—meaning all humans—and living beings in nature. Isn't it logical that if we feel good, we would want to share that feeling with others? Isn't that the right thing to do? I'm not talking about any sort of superficial spirituality. No. I'm talking about our responsibility to each other. The Jews have a term for it, *tikkun olam*. It means that we bear a responsibility not only for our own moral, spiritual, and material welfare, but also for the welfare of society at large. That's how I feel. That's why these healings are so meaningful to me.

WHM AND MULTIPLE SCLEROSIS

When I was diagnosed with multiple sclerosis (MS) in 2011, the ground beneath my feet subsided. Our fourth child was ten months old, and the symptoms affected my hand and arm, making it impossible for me to perform in my profession as a violinist. My neurologist told me that nothing would change and that I would have to learn to live with this handicap. But then my mother told me about Wim Hof.

I thought, *Let me just try.*

During the workshop, I already got tingling in my fingers during the breathing exercises.

So they weren't "dead" after all. There was life in them.

I called my husband at the time and said, "A miracle has happened."

From that day on, I continued to practice the WHM, and in a short amount of time, my hand and arm recovered 99 percent. The WHM has taught me to really listen to my body, which makes me powerful. Today my MS is under control; I am an active mother of five, work full time in the Netherlands Philharmonic Orchestra, train, and live life as I would like to live it. The WHM has made me strong both physically and mentally.

ANUSCHKA FRANKEN
AMSTERDAM, NETHERLANDS

Despite all the healing experiences people report, I know that skeptics remain. That's why I keep beating this drum and participating in studies and allowing myself to be used by scientists like some sort of human guinea pig. The result is that we now have a ton of data to support our claims. I'm not just diving into or falling into assumptions. I'm not extrapolating. I've established a base of verified knowledge that will survive me, just as my mission will. It's bigger than me. We all have a pathway to become happy, strong, and healthy, and it leads to the soul. Without the soul, we are just pieces of meat, but with the soul, we are eternal and indestructible. What is *your* mission? What is *your* vision quest? That vision quest is really you, the exploration of the still unventured terrain within yourself. That's why Native peoples do vision quests when they are young. You are now older, but that's no excuse. The oldest known WHM practitioner right now, who lives in the United States, is Frances Frederico. At ninety-seven years old, she learned about the method through an accredited program that brings the benefits of the Wim Hof Method to seniors. As of this writing, she's still on her quest. She's still following the light.[5]

Let me tell you a story. There's a man I've had the good fortune to get to know through this work. His name is Frans van Beers, and like Bertwin, he's a gardener by trade. He was seventy-six years old when I met him, but he looked (and still looks) much younger. He's got a great spirit. He comes to me one day and says he wants to climb Kilimanjaro. He has no experience in mountaineering whatsoever, and he's suffering from Lyme disease, but he is determined. So I agree to let him join our expedition. This is also the one that investigative journalist Scott Carney, who chronicled the experience in his book *What Doesn't Kill Us*, participated in. Frans impressed me so much with his motivated nature. He suffered from Lyme disease and had no mountaineering experience, but man, he was standing there in front of me with such a strength of mind and heart. I had no doubt that he could make it because I could see how switched on he was. And wouldn't you know it, Frans reached the summit with the second group, in just thirty hours. Not only was this unbelievable; it was unprecedented. Inspiring. But that is not the end of the story.

As it turns out, Frans's experience on the mountain was transformative. He came down a different man. He's now using his conviction, motivation, and the power of his mind to heal other people suffering from Lyme. He's showing them what's possible. He's taking them into

Frances Frederico practicing an adaptive form of cold exposure in a video training program for seniors[6]

the cold and walking them through the breathing, but more importantly, he's showing them the power of belief. He refused to allow his age or his disease to define him, and he's inspiring others to do the same. He's giving back and practicing, in his own way, *tikkun olam*, repairing the world. He's helping more people with Lyme disease than any doctor ever did. And two years later, he went back and summitted Kilimanjaro again, at the age of seventy-eight.

Recently I saw a photograph of Frans on Facebook. He was standing in an ice bath while holding two large kettlebells. And next to the picture there was a caption that read: "I will never retire." I loved it. Here is this man pushing eighty years old showing everyone else how to live. The man is an inspiration, a true spirit. I am proud to count him among my friends.

But among all the people I have taken up Kilimanjaro, perhaps none is more impressive or as inspirational as Anna Chojnacka. Two years before she reached Uhuru Peak at the top of Kilimanjaro, she was told by a doctor to get accustomed to the idea that she would be wheelchair-bound within five years due to the debilitating, irreversible effects of multiple sclerosis (MS).[7] Anna was (and is) a mother of three though, and she simply refused to accept that diagnosis. She came to me out of desperation, as a last hope. She told me her story, and I was moved. I said, "Hey, I'm going to climb Kilimanjaro in a few months. Are you coming with me? Be motivated." And she *was* motivated. Tell any mother of three that she's about to become wheelchair-bound, and you will see the true meaning of motivation. But there wasn't any doubt in her mind. No hesitation whatsoever. She was going to do it no matter what. Like Henk and Frans and a number of others who have undertaken these expeditions with me, she had no experience with cold exposure or with mountaineering, but neither of those things dissuaded her in the slightest. She was going to make it to the summit, in record time, out of the sheer force of her will. Mind you, this was our second expedition up Kilimanjaro, the one in which all the scientists and alpine experts told us was irresponsible, that people were going to die. But, of course, nobody died. We reached the summit in forty-four hours. And Anna? Eight years after her grim diagnosis, she's running marathons. She's given birth to a fourth child. And she wrote a memoir about her experience on the mountain entitled *Kilimanjaro als Medicijn* (*Kilimanjaro as Medicine*). She's as happy as she ever was.

Isn't that the goal? Happiness? Health? That's what I want for you and for anyone who reads this book; start by getting into the cold shower and breathing in the morning. Feel inspired to push past your own perceived limits, to get past your comfort zone, try something new like GP Jenny. And Henk. And Bertwin. And Frans. And Anna. And thousands and thousands of others whose lives have been transformed by these simple techniques. They're happy. They're healthy. They're alive and vibrant and reflecting the soul. So why not you? What else are you looking for? People today are so caught up in their egos, in the chase for material gain or status that they lose sight of who they really are. You're alive, man! Your soul is alive! Wake up! You can be strong without thoughts, just existing in the stillness of the mind, well-nourished with the life-force, the blood flow, because your thinking brain isn't dominating those resources. Breathe. Go out into the cold. Feel it. Follow the light. It will take you back into yourself.

You don't need external validation to try the method. You don't need anything, really, except love. Love will restore the beauty of life to your consciousness, and you will then reflect it. You will radiate it, and it will attract others like a beacon. That's what these stories of healing are about. Your blood flow, the life-force, the electricity, they're all in there. But what are you going to do with them? This is the only life you've got, so it's time to move beyond your conditioning. It's time to move beyond your fear or whatever else is holding you back from living fully because that's the way nature meant you to be. Your fears are a consequence of a conditioned mind, and they are nothing but a burden. Where would Henk be today if he had given into his fears? Where would Anna be?

The method is not a pill. You have to have dedication and conviction, to become your own teacher and guide. It makes you meet your fear rather than turn away from it. Once you become more comfortable with this new-found authority of yourself, you are able to gain momentum, and suddenly you want to eat better, you want to run a marathon, your dreams are revived.

Become like a child again — curious, safe. Hold your own hand through this process. Keep a diary, talk with your partner about it. The method is also about connection, empathy, and building bridges between us.

The letters and emails come in every day. "Thank you, Wim Hof," they say. "Thank you for what you did in my life. You changed it completely. I was on the verge of suicide, but now I'm happy. I got it! And I'm spreading it like wildfire. I'm totally motivated and into life."

This is what we have lost, the motivation for life itself. To realize that we are beautiful, all of us, and that's what we're doing here. We're bringing back an awareness of the beauty of life, consciously, to all the people, without dogma. We're divine beings and don't need a set of doctrines to bind us together, to spread love among each other, to help self-actualize and find happiness and health within ourselves. What else is there after that? When you find true happiness, you don't have longings for anything else, and you don't go and do anything that makes you unhappy. No. You *stay in the happiness*. You bask in it. And you share it. It is very powerful to do the method as a group. At our events we see people connecting on a very basic level, all simply present together in the now. That is powerful stuff! There's an old Dutch saying: "Sharing happiness is double happiness, and sharing sorrow is half sorrow." It may sound corny, but it's true. To me, making people feel better is the real purpose in my life. There is nothing that fills me up more than the betterment of any human. These people's stories are amazing. And how can I pay them back? By keeping on, by staying on course.

I'm a man on a mission, and I will not fail. Until I die, I will show all the people in the world that we were born to be not only wild, but to be happy, strong, and healthy. You don't even need to get too wild. The method will work for you even if you never take an ice bath, even if your breath retention never gets to two minutes, even if your cold shower never gets below 60 degrees. You can do the basic breathing practice without even getting out of bed.

The control I've gained through going into nature and coming back is a control that you too can gain with training. You can experience the true nature of yourself, the inner nature, the way nature meant it to be. I present it to you here in this book with these techniques that have held up to the scrutiny of researchers and scientists around the world. It's all here, just as you and I are here. You are me, and I am you. We are the soul, the light. We are bound by its energy, which is love. The love is as straight as an arrow, and I don't miss.

WHM AND BREAST CANCER

In 2015, I was diagnosed with an aggressive, rapidly dividing form of breast cancer that required six months of chemotherapy, six weeks of radiation, and a breast-saving operation. In between chemotherapy treatments, I started doing the breathing exercises, cold training, and concentration exercises that form the pillars of the Wim Hof Method, and when I saw my oncologist the next time, he looked at me with amazement after analyzing my blood results because my white blood cells had tripled in one week! Naturally I continued with the Wim Hof Method, and I ended up feeling less tired and more energetic than I had the whole previous year. I then decided that I wanted to share my knowledge and experience with the WHM with others, so a year later, I became a certified Wim Hof Method instructor. Now I hold workshops twice a month in my hometown of Ibiza, where I live in remission of my cancer. It brings me such joy to share my happiness with others and to see them benefit from the method as well. I'm truly blessed.

SUZANNE BOERSMA
IBIZA, SPAIN

8 WHM FOR PERFORMANCE

One of the greatest benefits of practicing my method is the incredible effect it has on one's athletic performance. Elite athletes from around the world—professionals, Olympians—come to me all the time to train. These athletes are supposed to represent the height of peak performance, but as impressive as they are, they don't. They come to me seeking more—something that can give them a competitive edge without having to resort to dangerous illegal drugs. And no matter what kind of shape they are in, I show them how they can be better and how they can do so naturally. Because even when they are achieving what appears to be peak performance, there's still room to improve their energy levels, endurance, mental focus, recovery time, and as a result, their overall athletic performance. And the way they do this is by changing their biochemistry.

Present within the cells of all forms of life is a chemical called adenosine triphosphate (ATP), which provides the energy to drive many biological processes, including, in humans, muscle contraction. ATP molecules do exist in cells that are in an anaerobic state, without the presence of oxygen, but they multiply exponentially in cells that are in an aerobic state, in the presence of oxygen.[1] The more ATP molecules, the more energy. And that energy is useful not only for enhanced athletic performance but also for increased muscular plasticity, which relates to a muscle's ability to alter its structural and functional properties in accordance with changes in environmental conditions. In the case of athletes, plasticity refers specifically to a muscle's ability to recover from stress. Athletes expend so much energy simply maintaining their bodies in the peak or near-peak condition they're already in, so they often lack the extra energy needed to repair their bodies, rehabilitate, and get into this plasticity mode.[2]

The process of creating more ATP molecules and thus generating more energy involves aerobic dissimilation, in which oxygen influences the physical mitochondrial process by breaking down the lactic acid that builds up in one's muscles during exercise.[3]

How can an athlete, whether they are elite or recreational, achieve this? By breathing. I advise the athletes I consult with to breathe more than they feel they need to and to think of it like a mantra. When you breathe more than you feel you need to, you can surpass your conditioning regardless of your VO_2 max, which is the measure of your maximum oxygen consumption during exercise. And when we are able to surpass our conditioning, we also gain an ability to overcome stressful situations and to rise beyond our perceived physical limitations. You don't need to be an elite athlete to accomplish this. You don't need to be an athlete at all, really. All you need to do is the conscious breathing you learned in chapter 4. Aerobic dissimilation creates about thirty times more ATP molecules than are created when there is no oxygen. Just breathe and feel the difference.

What kind of monster do you want to become? A super monster like the Incredible Hulk? These films and comic books explore fantasies that are based on unexplained (or unexplainable) realities. Think of the mother who lifts a car off a trapped child. She's no athlete let alone a superhero, but she is able to summon the power to lift thousands of pounds in an instant. This is a phenomenon known as hysterical strength, and it is often attributed to an increase in adrenaline production, though there is little evidence to support that. What we do know, however, is that these people somehow find the strength within to perform seemingly miraculous physical feats. What we don't know is how to tap into that energy. Until now.

I found a way, and it's coming from nature. From within you. It's knocking at your door right now.

The breath combined with the power of the mind can significantly increase the amount of ATP molecules and adrenaline in your cells. How much do you need? How much do you think you need? What level of performance will make you happy? I'm not suggesting that you do the breathing and then go outside and start lifting all the cars on your street. Competitive athletics have become a little bit crazy, I think. It's driving people mad. It's also driving them toward injury, burnout, and depression. I know Olympic gold medalists who became very depressed after their careers were over because they no longer had that competitive outlet to drive them. But what's the point of winning a gold medal if it doesn't make you happy?

This, again, is a symptom of a societal issue that has nothing whatsoever to do with the expression of our true nature, of our souls. This search for external validation, this need to be "the best," is truly a fool's errand. Being the best and being *the best you can be* are quite different things, see. But you can become the best version of yourself when you gain the ability to regulate your own biochemistry, your own energy, and to channel that energy however you see fit. How much energy do you want? If you learn to use your mind together with the breathing, you will be able to increase it exponentially. What you do with it after that is up to you, but the possibilities are endless.

WIM HOF METHOD AND PROFESSIONAL FOOTBALL

Say goodbye to performance anxiety and game-day jitters. The Wim Hof Method uses your body's own ability to recalibrate and refocus so you can perform at your peak.

In January 2020, I joined Wim Hof and a number of other authors and influencers for one of his expeditions in Poland. I already practice cold exposure, so it was the breathing part that was key for me. It was a life-changing experience. I now do the Wim Hof basic breathing every single morning, using the free app. All you have to do is lie in your bed and let Wim guide you. At the end of seventeen minutes, there is a recalibration in your mind, a chemical change in your brain from this breathing technique.

After the third round of breathing, I feel freaking great, like it gets my brain right for the day. Since the expedition, my sleep has dramatically improved, my recovery is off the charts, and because I'm hyper-saturated with oxygen in my body, I don't hit fatigue until a lot later when I'm training. I think there's an incredible application here for professional athletes. Quarterbacks, kickers, punters, guys who play a very focused, intensive position—imagine how much more effective they would be at controlling their heart rate and performing their skill when it matters most if they used this breathing protocol.

I don't want to just take care of my body. I don't want to just live longer. I want to be able to get more out of my body than anybody has, ever. But the method is not even about that. It's just about being able to access more of the gifts that God has given you, to help you gain a tool that helps you become your greater self. I think supplements and exercise are amazing, but I don't think anything is more amazing than doing this breath work first thing in the morning.

STEVE WEATHERFORD
SUPER BOWL CHAMPION, TENURE NFL VETERAN,
ENTREPRENEUR, HUSBAND, AND LOVING FATHER OF FIVE

Another benefit of the increased energy the method yields is a new-found ability to attack disease. When people are sick or suffering from chronic disease, the mere act of survival consumes all of the energy they have. They don't have the means to create more ATP molecules for repair, rehabilitation, or plasticity of the mind and body. That's why we have to introduce these mindful conscious breathing techniques to care facilities worldwide. Doing so will increase and accelerate patients' ability to repair their bodies, and they will feel a lot better than with pharmaceuticals. Aerobic dissimilation is all-natural, safe, and effective. It's done by the mind and the breath, and when they come together, you are able to create more energy for repair and rehabilitation, which in turn, makes you feel better. It's amazing how simple it is.

Of course, we need to keep investigating all of this through science because while what I'm saying here has already been proven by me and thousands of others, acceptance of these truths has not yet become widespread among the medical establishment. That's nothing new for me though, and it's one of the reasons why I decided to write this book. I'm grateful to my publisher for giving me this platform because it's powerful. We're changing lives and illuminating a path toward health and healing while we wait for the scientific community, which can sometimes be as slow as a turtle, to catch up to us. But it works, and there's data to back it up.

Viennese psychotherapist and breath therapist Wilfried Ehrmann, author of *The Manual of Breath Therapy*, wrote in a 2015 article, "With more breathing, there is simply more ATP, while the production of lactic acids is reduced, which keeps the body in an alkaline state. At the same time, with deeper breathing, more CO_2 is exhaled, the blood pH level becomes more alkaline, and thus more aerobic dissimilation can happen."[4]

When more aerobic dissimilation happens, energy increases, and it is here where, once again, the mind enters the equation. Remember, I was able to resist the stress of an endotoxin by the sheer power of my mind. After being exposed to the cold so many times, the neurological pathways in my brain were and remain well-established. I didn't even know this until I was tested in the lab at Radboud, but now I'm able to credibly advance this theory because the science backs it up. We did it. The mind, together with the breathing, can increase your energy levels much more than you ever thought was possible.

WHM PROTOCOL: POWER BREATHING FOR ENDURANCE

This exercise is an adaptation of the Basic Breathing Exercise to enhance athletic performance. You can delay the deprivation of oxygen in the muscle tissue, thereby postponing the point of lactic acidification, which leads to fatigue and failure. The breathing exercise causes a release of adrenaline and glucose that your body can absorb immediately and achieve better performance.

Before you begin an endurance exercise, such as long distance running or cycling, do three to four rounds of power breathing:

1 Breathe in deeply and relax to let your breath go sixty times.
2 On the last breath, inhale fully and then hold the breath for at least fifteen seconds (or as long as feels comfortable), squeeze your entire body toward the head by tensing your pelvic floor and allowing that pressurized feeling to move up your spine to the top of your head.
3 Relax to let your breath go and start a new round.
4 Start each new round with your regular WHM breathing rhythm, and then increase the speed and intensity of your breathing as the round proceeds. This increase is what makes this power breathing.
5 Wait a couple of minutes to ground yourself again and then begin your endurance exercise.
6 Breathe more than you feel is necessary and stay aware of your breath during the endurance exercise.

You've got all the energy you need to do anything, to overcome any obstacle or disease in your body, life, path, or destiny. That's the way we were equipped by nature. Adenosine triphosphate, aerobic dissimilation, mitochondrial processes, the citric acid cycle — whatever you want to call it — just get your energy. There's plenty, more than you'll ever need. How much do you want? I tell the athletes I advise to breathe more than they feel is needed. And you know what they say to me? They say, "Within a week of doing the breathing, after years at what I believed was the limit of my performance, I suddenly increased my energy by 10, 15 percent or more." That's why I always say "Breathe, motherfuckers." Sorry, it's "French," but I know you understand. Just breathe and you will see amazing results.

The Radboud University study proved for the first time that we are able to consciously influence the mitochondrial processes in our lymphatic systems. Scientists had developed a way to measure them with a laser, but they didn't know how to influence them at will, how to do it physically. And because with our conscious breathing we are accelerating the mitochondrial processes and thus our energy levels in the lymphatic system, we are able to rid our bodies of toxins and other waste faster and more efficiently. In addition to circulating lymph fluid, which returns proteins and fats to the bloodstream throughout the body, the lymphatic system also functions as a kind of waste-management system on a cellular level. But because we could not enter into this system physically, we weren't previously able to activate those mitochondrial processes to create more energy to get rid of the garbage — the toxins — that had stored up in our cells. And now, through conscious breathing and the aerobic dissimilation it brings about, we can. So, beyond the performance and restorative benefits, the breathing also helps to cleanse the body of harmful substances. It's a trinity.

Dutch mixed martial arts superstar Alistair "the Demolition Man" Overeem is one of the elite athletes who is benefiting from this trinity. One of only two fighters to hold world titles in both MMA and K-1 kickboxing at the same time, Overeem has been fighting professionally

UFC superstar Alistair Overeem credits the Wim Hof Method with improving his conditioning.

since 1999. Now forty, he's reached an age at which most fighters have retired, but Overeem shows no signs of slowing down. As of this writing he's the number-six-ranked heavyweight in the Ultimate Fighting Championship, and he credits the Wim Hof Method with improving his conditioning.[5]

When, in 2015, Overeem faced former UFC Heavyweight Champion Junior dos Santos (then the number-one-ranked heavyweight in the UFC), he dealt with his prefight nerves by returning to the breathing exercises he had been practicing daily after beginning to train with me earlier that year. That helped him to remain calm and focused on the task at hand, which was a fight against a truly formidable opponent, a knockout artist who had compiled a ring record of 17–3 up to that point. But Alistair stepped into the Octagon in Orlando, Florida, that night and took care of business, dispatching dos Santos by virtue of a technical knockout at the end of the second round. And while a heavyweight prizefight of this magnitude is an extremely taxing affair, he reported afterward that he wasn't tired. His cardio had improved significantly as a result of our training.

But increased aerobic capacity isn't the only benefit the method provides to athletes. It also helps them to recover faster. After every workout, whether it is cardio or weight training (or, in Overeem's case, a prizefight), an athlete's body needs time to recover properly. Muscle tissue gets damaged, and energy stores are depleted during exercise, and as a result, their body requires rest. Athletes who practice the method report better sleep, reduced inflammation, and faster recovery times. We have recently shown, in a study published while writing this book, that the breathing activates the cori cycle, recycling the lactic acid, via pyruvate, into new glucose.[6] That's more energy! That's a more efficient practice. It's therefore no wonder that Alistair Overeem believes this method can "change the world."

But you do not need to be an elite athlete to gain these same benefits. If average people suffering from such maladies as multiple sclerosis, rheumatoid arthritis, and cancer can make it to the summit of Mount Kilimanjaro, just imagine what the method can do for the casual joggers, Sunday-league footballers, and pick-up hoopsters among us. If your goal is to run, say, a nine-minute mile, which for a man in his fifties is a sign of moderate fitness, then certainly an increase in your aerobic capacity can help you to accomplish that.[7] The same goes for Sunday-league and pick-up ballers. If your level of cardiovascular fitness is preventing you from being able to run the length of the field or court without getting winded, try to envision what you might be able to do with increased amounts of oxygen. This isn't to suggest that you will suddenly morph into the second coming of Lionel Messi or LeBron James, but you will see a marked improvement in your endurance and, in turn, your enjoyment of the game. This enjoyment will only be heightened when you later find that the aches, pains, and fatigue that usually follow a strenuous athletic effort are greatly reduced as well.

WIM HOF METHOD EXPERIMENT #3

DOES WHM IMPROVE YOUR ATHLETIC PERFORMANCE?

To demonstrate the power of the technique, let's do some push-ups. First, do as many push-ups as you can to set a baseline. Most of us can only do ten or twenty before becoming seriously fatigued. Now do a single round of the Basic Breathing Exercise, exhale fully, and try the push-ups again during the retention phase, with your breath held out on the exhale. If you feel you can, keep doing the push-ups after you breathe in for the recovery breath. You may be surprised to learn that suddenly you can do twice, three times, or four times as many as you did before.

Dr. Mehmet Oz isn't an elite athlete, but the sixty-year-old surgeon turned popular talk show host is reasonably fit for a man of his age. Still, when Scott Carney visited his show in promotion of his book on the method and walked Oz (and two audience members) through the breathing, Oz shocked his viewers and himself by dropping down and doing nearly forty push-ups.

"It's interesting," Oz said on the telecast. "I don't even feel tired. I could keep going. And that's not how many push-ups I could normally do, by the way. That's a lot more than is the norm. That was *crazy* effective. And my heart rate's not even up."[8]

If a nonathlete like Oz can bang out forty push-ups after doing just one round of Wim Hof breathing one time, just think of what you might be able to do after multiple rounds following a sustained period of consistent practice. Push-ups are only the beginning, and you are limited only by the depth of your imagination. What would you like to do?

I'm sixty-one years old now, but I feel much younger. I'm as fit as some men half my age. What is age, anyway? I feel young because I *am* young. The spirit and soul are eternal and exist outside of time. They acknowledge no limitations. So I press on. I advance. I still do my ice bath every single day because I love it. It's brought me into a deeper understanding of myself and my place in the universe, within nature, and for that I am grateful. The ice bath has been especially helpful of late as I have been doing a certain kind of muscular training to see if I'm able to deacidify my biochemistry even more, to become even more alkaline, which will enable me to go further into myself and beyond, achieving a biochemical state in which there is no acid at all, no sourness. How do I do it? With my mind. I set my mind so that its neurology has a direct influence on my physical performance.

For example, for exercise, I do stretches with a resistance band. I put the band over a door, and then I pull down. I used to only be able to do about 50 reps before growing tired, but now I can do 160 without ever really fatiguing my muscles. Despite these gains, my muscles aren't really growing. That's not the point of the exercise anyhow. No. I'm influencing the acidic state of my muscle tissue—increasing my lactate threshold—by using my mind, together with the breathing, to extend the muscle's power. You don't need big muscles to generate power. Bigger isn't always better, and in fact, sometimes it's worse. Look at the bodies of endurance athletes like cyclists and long-distance runners. Their muscles are lean, but they are able to generate tremendous power. Lactic acid builds up in our muscles during intense exercise, causing fatigue, pain, and, eventually, failure. Elite athletes have higher lactate thresholds than average, and those who practice my method can achieve similar results, with or without the benefit of superior genetics.

WHM AND SEXUAL PERFORMANCE

Athletic performance isn't the only kind of performance that is enhanced by practicing the method. If it can enable a man to drop down and do forty push-ups after just one round, imagine how it might benefit you between the sheets. Jelle Steenbeek, creator of the Lionwood program, is a WHM instructor who has found that practicing WHM breathing with his sexual partner enhances the experience for them both.

Ever since I've been instructing the Wim Hof Method, I've been using it to upgrade all kinds of facets of daily life. One of my favorites is to use breathwork to elevate the sexual experience. I've found that the state of mind it generates, in combination with the extra energy created in your cells for longer stamina, and the activation of primordial powers from our lizard brain, can make for some serious fireworks.

Holding my spouse by the chest while sitting behind her against some pillows and doing three or four rounds of breathing requires that we are both on the same team. I've found that this is a unique and tender way to align with my partner.

WHM practice also trains my perineal muscle each time I "squeeze" in the second retention of a breath cycle. This is one of the most important muscles for a good sex life, for both men and women.

Another thing breathing helped me to do is slow down and give my partner more time to enjoy herself. As a man, if you get heated and keep going, it is very likely you'll orgasm if you go beyond 80 percent of excitement. If you stop each time you are there and don't go over the edge, you are able to get to much higher states of orgasmic joy. At each "plateau," you stop at 80 percent, do the breathing, and start over. You don't start again from zero; you have a higher base to launch from, which gets you higher. Plus, more feeling over your body is more control over your equipment.

Don't even get me started on ice baths in relation to better sex and children named after Wim!

JELLE STEENBEEK
BELGISCH PARK, NETHERLANDS

Diet plays a role in our performance of course, but it's not everything. Recently, at a retreat at my training camp in Poland, someone said to me, "Yeah, I see you sometimes taking a drink." I said, "Like a beer? I'm not a puritan, man. A little beer once in a while is beautiful. I like it. Not too much, but in moderation, yes. Beer is lovely." I'm committed to my mission, but I'm no paragon of virtue. I'm not here to be an example for you, but instead to be the master within myself. Let *that* be the example for others to emulate. We only go through this life once, and we might as well enjoy ourselves while we do. Those who would deprive themselves of simple pleasures like an occasional beer may benefit from it in terms of their short-term performance, but they aren't nourishing the soul.

I said to the guy, "You know what? I'm going to attempt to set a new world record now. Without training or any advanced preparation, I'm going to stand barefoot in the snow for three hours in a horse stance. I'm going to show you how to control that which becomes acidic so it does not become acidic, so I can keep on performing and not tire. But before I do that, I want a beer."

I don't know if you are familiar with the horse stance, which is an important stance in the martial arts, but it's a rather difficult position to hold. Just trying to hold it for a couple of minutes is a challenge, let alone three hours. Lactic acid builds up in the muscles, primarily the quadriceps, very quickly, and then fatigue and soreness set in. Holding a horse stance for three hours requires much more than an ability to withstand and abide pain. It requires control over the biochemistry inside the muscles. That's real performance. That's detoxifying muscle that is actively engaged in intoxicating exertion.

Using my breathing and harnessing the power of my mind, I set the record.[9] Then, afterward, if only to prove my point further, I said, "Now I want another beer." And I had one.

WIM HOF METHOD EXPERIMENT #4

HOW LONG CAN YOU HOLD A HORSE STANCE?

How long can you hold a horse stance, with or without beer? Let's find out!

To get into a horse stance, stand up straight, then spread your feet apart, about one and a half times the width of your shoulders. Make sure that your feet are facing forward, your spine is straight, and your posture is upright and aligned. Now bend your knees into a squat, lowering your upper body as if you were on horseback. Keep your knees in line with your toes. Place your hands on your hips. And hold.

Doing deep breathing will help, as it lessens the build-up of lactic acid in your muscles, which leads to fatigue and failure. First breathe regularly and see how long you can hold the stance. Then, the second time around, breathe deeply and evenly and see the difference it makes. I also like to add arm movements and sounds — pushing my right hand away from my body to the left side, then switching to push out with my left hand to the right side, making "Hoo-Hah" sounds as I breathe. In our WHM retreats, we often use this exercise to stay warm after being in cold water. With energy of the group to carry them, people are easily able to hold the stance for thirty minutes.

Performance comes from the feeling that you have all the energy you need to achieve your goal. For that you need sleep, less stress, the food that is right for you, but you also need the right biochemistry, the right breathing. You need to give your body the right tools for recovery, otherwise you can easily put yourself at risk.

To me, performance is life itself. If you live your life, feel well, and follow your passion from the heart, then who can stop you? If you don't do things with passion, with your heart, and with your emotions, then you are just running on adrenaline. You will burn out. If you are able to handle your stress mechanisms, your performance will be whole-hearted. Your breath gives you the ability to connect with yourself when you are in competitive performance, while stress and strain can make you disconnect. Cleanse yourself every day with the method. It's about the emotion, the connection with your heart, the will to play, the joy, the ease that comes from that. Your heart is the reason you do all this. It always has to remain on top. This goes deeper than your story of yourself. What is true success? Living in your heart.

9
THE TRUTH IS ON OUR SIDE

We are the new gladiators. You and me. The old gladiators are no more, and their wars are over. Their problems are not your problems. Your life is yours. My ideas are not radical, and I'm not superhuman or extraordinary, but I've got a strong belief that we are able to change the world. I believe it because I see the power of the method in my real life every day. I live it. I live *for* it. With every experiment, every publication, we're rewriting the books, making our case. We're operating beyond the known limits of science.

I remember once meeting with Professor Maria Hopman in a library after she had experimented on me. I had all these bold assumptions about how to change science, and she said, "Wim, look around, all these books, do you see? If what you say is true, we'll have to change all these books!" And you know what? They *do* have to change the books now because they're obsolete. The science has evolved, man. The content has changed. *We've* changed.

But all of that is external. The cold and the breath haven't changed. Humans have battled the cold since the very first winter, and Tibetan monks have been practicing conscious breathing techniques for more than a thousand years. You breathe more than twenty-three thousand times a day without even thinking about it at all. But when you breathe with intention, it kindles an evolutionary instinct, which, whether conscious or unconscious, heightens the experience.

After our triumph at Radboud, we saw a bit of a spike in interest in what we are doing, but mostly among journalists. There were a few television appearances and articles, but it was minimal compared to what I was expecting. Some even continued to frame our story as a curiosity and me as some sort of genetic anomaly or outlier, but the research had been published, and with that came a measure of credibility. There are always going to be cynics and skeptics pushing back against you when you challenge the established order of things. Those cynics mock what they do not understand because they fear it. They fear the truth. I took advantage of the momentum we were building by engaging in more research.

Back in 2009, under the supervision of Dr. Wouter van Marken Lichtenbelt and his team in the Nuclear Medicine Department at Maastricht University in the Netherlands, I showed that I possessed, at fifty-two years old, the same amount of brown fat (or brown adipose tissue — BAT) in my body that young adults do, even though the common belief at the time was that BAT is no longer present in adults.[1] Not only that, I metabolized four and a half times more energy from my brown fat than the other, far younger test subjects did.

In babies, brown fat plays a key role in both thermoregulation and thermogenesis, creating heat when little babies become cold because they're not able to move around as much as we do. Instead of depositing energy like white fat does, brown fat is capable of energy combustion. As we grow older, the amount of brown fat in our bodies decreases sharply. This is partially due to our wearing clothes all the time and dwelling within climate-controlled bubbles of our own design. But just as muscle atrophies from lack of use, so do our stores of BAT, which diminish when our bodies are not activated or stimulated by the cold. This is why older people were believed to not carry much, if any, BAT in their bodies.

But by now you surely know that I am not like most people my age. Or any age. And because I had been going into the cold and stimulating my body on a regular basis for many years, the researchers at Maastricht found the same amount of brown fat in my body as would normally be carried by a teenager. But what was more interesting to them than the presence of BAT in my body was the way that I was able to use it to generate heat. BAT activity was observed in twenty-three of the twenty-four test subjects (96 percent) during cold exposure, but I was the only subject who was able to activate his BAT to generate enough heat to maintain his core body temperature throughout the duration of the cold exposure without shivering.

The professors at Maastricht believed that they had discovered the secret of the Iceman—aha!—and they published their findings in the *New England Journal of Medicine*, which is the oldest continuously published peer-reviewed medical journal in the world. While my production of BAT plays a role in my ability to endure the cold, it does not tell the whole story. Because, as I later showed at Wayne State, I can generate heat via the intercostal muscle, but also by channeling the power of my mind, without breathing exercises. Professsor van Marken Lichtenbelt suggested that muscle contraction may have played a role in the generation of heat, but the idea of will alone was unknown territory.[2]

Because they couldn't quite figure out how I am able to do the things I do, they brought me and my identical twin brother, Andre, in for a comparative study a few years later.[3] They wanted to determine, definitively, whether or not we were, indeed, the genetic anomalies they suspected we were or if, instead, my abilities were the result of training. Andre is a truck driver by trade, so he lives a somewhat sedentary life compared to me. He wasn't practicing the method back then (he is now) though he had an awareness of its techniques. He wasn't yet taking ice baths or doing the specialized breathing techniques I had developed, but he was and remains quite active outside of his work and frequently enjoyed open-water swimming, which could account for the stores of brown fat Professor van Marken Lichtenbelt's team detected in him. Still, genetically, biologically, we are the same. We're essentially genetic copies of each other, with no discernible phenotypic differences.

Much to the consternation of the researchers at Maastricht, that's exactly what they discovered. Reporting their findings in the peer-reviewed, open-access scientific journal PLOS One, they wrote, "No significant differences were found between the two subjects."[4] How then can it be that I am able to do the things I can do and Andre cannot?

If, after all the testing, we were found to be the same, the only logical answer is that it must be the intensity of my training and the ways my body copes with it. After decades of training in the cold, I have developed a different neurology. That's the power of the mind.

I speak of logic because this isn't magic. The research being conducted on the method is done in the interest of furthering our understanding of human potential. It's the new paradigm in science, and the more people who participate in and read these studies, whether they be medical professionals or just everyday folks, the more we advance our cause. We can no longer be so narrow-minded in our approach to things, but instead see the bigger picture. Nature is showing us that we cannot trap the knowledge, we have to *be* the knowledge. We can't just say that if you possess BAT, you will be able to withstand it all. No. You need your *mind* in it. Realizing the true extent of the power of the mind is just developing neurological pathways that contribute to a new reality. This is the holy trinity: cold as a mirror, breath as the guide, and mindset as the creator.

In collaboration with researchers at the Royal Melbourne Institute of Technology (RMIT) in Australia, we conducted a survey study with more than three thousand subjects. Respondents to the researchers' questionnaire included more than a hundred who claimed that the method helped them alleviate or eliminate the symptoms of arthritis. Another fifty responded that the method helped drive their cancer into remission. Many more reported relief of their chronic pain. The response, in a word, was overwhelming.

WHM AND CHRONIC PAIN

My life changed when a medical mistake was made during an artificial hip operation. Additional surgeries did not improve my situation, and I suffered from chronic pain and physical limitations every single day. But then I was introduced to the Wim Hof Method, and my life changed completely.

It provided me with the insights and skills I needed to improve the quality of my life fundamentally, despite the pain and limitations.

Pain is a complex phenomenon that can have a penetrating effect on life. Daily pain often results in a negative spiral that can lead to depression, isolation, and a reliance on medication. It can have an adverse effect on one's work and relationships. But employing the WHM enabled me to stop taking medication and instead influence my pain in a natural way. Concentration, breathing, and cold training allows me to produce the morphine-containing hormones and cannabinoids that reduce the experience of the pain. Pain may be a fixed value in life, but it is possible to control it with the Wim Hof Method.

WIEBE OTTEN
AMSTELVEEN, NETHERLANDS

BREATHING FOR PAIN REGULATION

When practicing the WHM for pain regulation, you're consciously manipulating your body and the pain you feel through the use of the breathing techniques.

1 Begin by sitting or lying down in a comfortable position. Once you are relaxed, direct your attention to the spot where you feel the pain. Then take five calm, deep breaths.
2 Now take twenty more deep breaths. Fully in, and letting go. Do not force your breath.
3 Exhale the last breath fully out, then inhale fully in once more, and hold it for ten seconds.
4 While holding the breath, focus your attention on the point of pain, and press your held breath toward it. Tense the muscles around the pain area as well.
5 Release your breath and all tension.

Think of the painful sensation as a signal. Motivate yourself to listen to this signal and become attuned to it. This signal tells you that the chemistry in this area needs to change, or is changing. A positive train of thought or mindset influences the perception of pain. The purpose is not to suppress the pain signal, but to change the internal chemistry that causes the pain in the first place.

I have now participated in dozens of studies with the researchers at Radboud University and other leading scientific institutions around the world, with great results. And in addition to the headline-grabbing discovery that humans are able to consciously influence our autonomic nervous, endocrine, and immune systems, we have also shown the benefit of the method as a natural treatment for a host of diseases, conditions, and disorders.

Have you ever heard of the inflammatory disease axial spondylitis, or AS? It's a scary-sounding disease, and for good reason, as it can cause some of the small bones in your spine to fuse together.[5] This significantly hinders one's flexibility and can result in a hunched-forward posture. If AS affects the ribs, it can also make deep breathing quite difficult. AS affects approximately 2.7 million Americans, with more than two hundred thousand new cases being reported each year. It has no known cure, and it is, of course, quite painful. But a team of researchers at the Academic Medical Center (AMC), the university hospital affiliated with the University of Amsterdam, led by Dr. Dominique Baeten, conducted a clinical trial in 2016 and 2017 in which twenty-four subjects between eighteen and forty-five years of age reported a significant reduction in inflammation and pain and an improvement in their general quality of life after a thirty-day immersion in the method.[6] The trial was such a success that the AMC now recommends the method as an official "add-on" therapy for those suffering from AS.

Dr. Matthias Wittfoth is a German neuroscientist and self-proclaimed stress-hacker who is now also a certified level-three WHM instructor. In 2018 Dr. Wittfoth attended the Reden Reicht Nicht ("Talking Is Not Enough") conference in Bremen. This annual conference brings neuroscientists from around the world together to discuss ways, beyond standard cognitive therapy, to bring relief and comfort to those suffering from depression and other mental and emotional conditions.

The researchers were interested to see if perhaps the method could help those who were emotionally blocked by increasing the neural activity in their brains. Would you like to know what happened with the brain scans? They showed that while doing the breathing exercises, their brains lit up like a disco ball. The blood flow went everywhere. The method, as we have discussed, brings back the blood flow to the brain and, with it, the neuroactivity it needs to prevent or ameliorate mental disorders. An official study is still necessary, and we still need to learn about the intricacies of the brain, but that was an extremely encouraging finding. If we truly are able to reverse or significantly curtail depression without pharmacological intervention, we can fundamentally change the way mental health care is practiced around the world. That's not an overstatement, guys. Just think about it.

The research continues to progress and evolve of course. This is an exciting time, and I am so very hopeful about our future. By the time you read this, there's a good chance we will have furthered our scientific understanding of the method's benefits even more. I don't doubt it.

In New Zealand, at Waikato University's School of Health, Stacy Sims, PhD, and (Chris) Martyn Beaven, PhD, began a study (since shelved due to a lack of funding) to determine the method's effectiveness in treating endometriosis. Endometriosis is an often-painful disorder in which tissue similar to the tissue that normally lines the inside of a woman's uterus grows outside of her uterus. In addition to the pain associated with the disorder, those suffering from endometriosis often encounter infertility issues. The Mayo Clinic reports that approximately one-third to one-half of women with endometriosis have had difficulty getting pregnant.[7]

The research at Waikato will be based on strong anecdotal evidence that the method's ability to reduce inflammation in the body can not only provide pain relief for endometriosis sufferers but also increase their chances of conceiving. I mention this study and all of these others not to stroke my ego or to say, "I told you so." I'm not even trying to convince you anymore because if you have read this far, chances are that you have already begun to reach a new understanding of what you thought may be possible. You're a new gladiator. Your shield is the method, and your sword is the truth. I hope that you will take what you have learned from this book and spread the message far and wide.

In that, you will fulfill our mission. But it's important, when you speak about the method, that you make it clear, especially when engaging more conservative minds, that everything is supported by science and that research is ongoing.

All of these studies point in the same direction. They show that we have far more influence over disease, both mentally and physically, than we ever thought possible. There are many more studies coming up, but how many do we need to publish before the scientific establishment acknowledges their findings? I don't know how any doctor could look at findings like these and not be intrigued enough to investigate further. This isn't something you can dismiss by citing a small sample size, or by writing me off as some sort of anomaly. Could it be that the idea of another way, a way that challenges their assumptions and that does not rely on pharmacology, is a threat to them? Could it be that they view the method in opposition to their own commercial interests? I would prefer not to think that way of course. I would like to believe that our goals are aligned, that we can work in concert for the benefit of mankind. Is this not what is at the heart of the Hippocratic Oath all physicians must pledge?

But are we into healing, or are we into medicine? That's what I am asking. If we are into healing, then let's get to it. Here's all this data. Let's go. It's kind of like that saying, "They tried to bury us, but we are the seeds." The truth of what we are doing cannot be buried. Sooner or later, these seeds will blossom. It cannot be controlled or repressed because it is free. It's not me. I'm just the messenger. It's science. And I welcome any doubter, any skeptic among the medical establishment to *prove me wrong*. I'm not afraid of criticism. No. Quite to the contrary, I think criticism polishes the diamond of truth. We've got the truth on our side, and it's a sufficient weapon in the war of ideas.

10 A DAY IN THE LIFE OF THE ICEMAN

I'm a father of six. The four oldest children, from my first marriage, work with me. Enahm is thirty-seven now; Isabelle is thirty-five; Laura, thirty-three; and Michael, thirty-two. They work with me every day, and I'm honored. It's a privilege to work with your children. When they were little and I would go to the primary school, they wanted me to act normally, but of course I was doing handstands and wearing T-shirts in the wintertime. The other parents would see me and say, "Look at him! He's crazy!" And that was embarrassing for the children. But now everything has switched; they serve the same mission. They see health turnarounds every day. Not just one or two, but dozens, hundreds, I don't know how many.

We work with another half-dozen people in the office, so the operation consists of about ten people altogether. I am so grateful not to be alone any longer in this. I was so used to being the black sheep, the crazy guy. What a blessing it is to have more hearts on board. Now I have a wonderful, beautiful, crazy, mischievous little two-year-old with my partner, Erin. He exudes an almost mystic cuteness when he walks around with his face all like this or like that, and I just melt. Me the Iceman. I melt all the time in his presence. I love him so much.

I also have a son that I have not seen in a long time. He is eighteen years old now. My breakup with his mother really affected me. I was quite down because of it. I was able to perform well, to do all the world-record attempts and everything, but it definitely cast a large shadow over me. At this point I have made a certain peace with it. I have found love again, and I am blessed not just with my own family but the larger family. I love the community we are building. I love life in general—to be honest, I'm crazy for it—but these things are like cherries on top of the cake. I've been blessed with many cherries. My life hasn't always been easy, and I'm well-acquainted with pain, but I'm happy. I'm as happy as I've ever been. It's true.

But there is still much work to do because there is misery in the world. We are on track with science to show that the human body and mind are capable of doing truly extraordinary things, and that the method is a conduit to it. Most of us still think that disease and illness, both physical and mental, are normal or, worse, inevitable, and that we are powerless to do anything about it. But disease and illness aren't normal, and you *can* do something about them. And now we can, I tell you, we can. We can change our DNA, engage the deepest parts of our brain, influence our immune system, our lymphatic system, and our nervous system, consciously. We've reversed autoimmune conditions, enhanced athletic performance, and more. We proved it. And now it's my job to spread the word.

I hold strong to my mission, and I believe in its power, but I'm not dogmatic about it. I'm no puritan. On the contrary, I believe that you should live life as you feel. Intuition and gut feelings have been repressed by dogma and doctrine for too long. New scientific evidence shows that we are much more capable than we have thought of controlling our stress and inflammation, our moods and emotions. We can become more accountable, more responsible, more able to identify what is good for us and what is not. We are like a computer that needs a reset.

I was alone for five years after I lost Olaya, with no partner. Was I lonely? Of course, and I felt a lot of sadness, but I had four kids. There was no time to be lonely. Waking up at 4:00 a.m., doing my breathing for an hour, that helped me cleanse myself, to grieve. When you have four kids, you are right there with them, not anywhere else. I had the

Getting to work every day with my four eldest children — Enahm, Isabelle, Laura, and Michael — is a great privilege

energy to be there for them because of the method. It allows you to feel renewed every morning, ready to meet the day with ease and joy and sense of openness. It trains you to be flexible in life.

It may sound like a contradiction, but those who are truly in control are the most free. That's why I don't think so much about what I'm doing; I just do it. I tap into the energy of the universe and reach beyond my ego. I let go. I make sure to feel the presence of the soul and to radiate it through genuine gratitude and happiness. I do this every single day, and it enables me to serve my family, my animals, and everybody and everything connected with the mission. A man on a mission is always awake inside, spiritually, to help others. That's what I do every day. Everything I do is in service of my mission, but still I'm free.

I want the same for you and for everyone who walks beside me on this journey. This book is a part of that, and so are all the other things I am doing to help spread this message. Life is crazy and beautiful and full of opportunity, and every day I seize it. Podcasts. Documentaries. Magazine features. Whatever it takes, I'm into it.

The more the message spreads, the more the scientists come calling too. From Melbourne to Hanover, Los Angeles to Michigan, to here in the Netherlands, scientists and researchers are investigating the method, putting it to the test and publishing their findings. I love science and welcome their inquiries, even the skeptics (*especially* the skeptics!) because they validate the truth of what we've been doing. There's only one truth, you know, and there's no conjecture, no snake oil to be sold. My mission is to share the love, share the light, and bring solutions not only to help others but also to solve the problems of the past. I think the time has come for us to wake up and say, "The nonsense of the past is no more because we're stopping it right now. We're standing up. We don't have to live like this anymore."

We are here, alive and in charge of our destiny. That charge is light, it's electricity, it's who we are, what we are. I wake up to an awareness of that every day, and it's motivating. People are so confused, so caught up in their thoughts, that they can't get out of their own way. They don't even know that they are blocking their own light. But I say just be happy, strong, and healthy. The rest is bullshit. It just confuses your mind. It's time to break free from all that, time for our spirits to bloom and express themselves in all their splendor.

Showing people how to access their light is a big part of what I do during the day, but besides that, of course, I breathe. I get high on my own supply. It's your supply too, remember, because we are all connected. Breathing changes your cellular construction, the molecular structures. It changes everything. It brings the light; it creates the right biochemistry within the body for the light to appear. Breathing marks the beginning of life, and it will show you the way to health and happiness. I know this because it happened for me and for so many others who have practiced the method. By now you probably think I sound like a broken record, and perhaps that is so. I don't care. Repetition is the mother of learning, and I'm banging the drum.

GET HIGH ON YOUR OWN SUPPLY

People ask me all the time what I think about weed. I think weed is great. Cannabinoids have many helpful benefits. But if you are able to get high on your own supply, that's even better, don't you think? So while weed is nice, I prefer to breathe and get into the cold. We have scientifically proven that the endocannabinoid system can be consciously activated. Do the breathing protocol, embrace the cold, and access the endocannabinoids in the deepest part of your brain. That's where the best weed is: inside. We can grow it in our own minds.

I rise in the morning, and I do my breathing. I don't do it because it's *good for me*, which it is, but because it *feels good*. That's why I *want* to do it. And then, shortly after, I take my cold shower, or an ice bath if I can. I love it, and I never skip a day, even when I am on the road. The ice bath, combined with the breathing, generates a ton of metabolic activity in the body. I stay in the cold water until I feel a deep peace, which comes from complete adaptation. I'm at rest, just looking around, and I'm charging up. My body is in a deeply stimulated metabolic state, because it has to work to withstand the cold. This makes me feel alive, with an absolute sense of being present—"I am here." I know all that, so I just do it, and it feels great. When I get out of the water, I don't jump directly into a warm shower or anything like that. No. I let the body work, and it's amazing what it does, what it can do. All the metabolic activity and biochemical processes are priming the body for ultimate functionality. Everything works. I do some stretching, some splits, some balance exercises. I'm in my sixties, and I can still balance my entire body weight on one arm. That might seem impressive, but I know that ten years from now—when I'm in my seventies, a senior citizen—I'll still be attempting to set all kinds of records and succeeding, just as I always have.

You know why? Because, like the rabbit in nature, we are built to perform. There are no elder homes for rabbits, you know. They're mammals just as we are mammals. And rabbits of advanced age are still able to flee, fight, find food, and mate. It's in their nature, and what else is there? Nature provided rabbits with all these tools for survival, and the same abilities are innate within us as well. We're built to survive and to thrive, so that's what I think I'm going to do until I die. Until the day I die, I will be able to flee, fight, find food, withstand the cold, handle my emotions, and make love. Is that all possible? The five F's: freeze, flight, fight, food, and fuck? I believe it is, and it's beautiful. It's who we are. We're not these hollow vessels staring at a tiny screen in our hand. We're not the lethargic couch potato watching the football match. How do you feel? I feel fucking nice! That's the way I choose to live my life every day.

Whatever it takes, I want to feel that this body is serving me. So I do my splits, suspend my body on one arm, balance on or hang from one finger even. My middle finger, naturally. I still hold the world record for that, you know. I hung from a rope tied between two hot air balloons back in February of 2003. We were more than mile up, and it was very cold. I wasn't wearing a shirt, and I lost the dexterity in my finger, my extremities. But still there I was, hanging by my middle finger for 23.5 seconds like some kind of lunatic. It was on television, and you can still find the clip on YouTube.[1] I've been able to do that and a lot of other crazy things with this body of mine. It's amazing, really. But even when the stunt is dangerous, which it often is, I always feel in control. Perhaps even more so. And that gives me a feeling more intense than any daredevil thrill. Like the cold water, it makes me feel truly alive.

Once you get a taste of that feeling, you crave it. You chase it. You can't get enough of it. You're like a man on a mission — never asleep, always available, always alert. Every single day, no matter how long it takes.

WHM PROTOCOL: ICE BATHS AND COLD PLUNGES

Getting into the cold in nature—there is nothing like it. And taking an ice bath is an amazing way to show yourself what you are capable of. To befriend the cold at home or in the wild, follow these steps:

1 First, find someone to share this experience with you. Ice baths and cold plunges are safer and more fun with friends.

2 Prepare yourself by doing one or two rounds of the basic breathing exercise as you visualize the cold water. How will it make you feel? Imagine how you will enter the water, be it a bathtub or a lake, and how you will feel when you do it. Assume a can-do mindset.

3 Confidently enter the water while taking deep, calm breaths. Focus on your breath. Embrace the cold; let it take you to the depths of yourself. Do NOT perform the WHM basic breathing technique. Instead, do long, conscious, exhalations to bring your breath into a controlled, steady rhythm. Take deep breaths through the nose and try to relax. Try letting out a long "Hummmmm" on the exhale.

4 Keep your focus on your breath and your being as you exit the water. Warm up by doing the horse stance exercise while maintaining your inner attention. (See page 118.)

The cold is our warm friend, our mirror, and our teacher. It can also be dangerous. When you extend exposure to the cold by going into an ice bath or open body of water, it is an intense experience. If you want to try an ice bath or a cold plunge, make sure you are being safe and smart about it. For a thorough training in safe cold exposure, please visit wimhofmethod.com to sign up for one of our courses or workshops.

11

FREEING OUR ANCESTRAL BURDEN

Each of us carries an ancestral burden within our genetic code. A 2018 research paper published in the *Proceedings of the National Academy of Sciences of the United States of America* by three members of the Economics of Aging Program at the National Bureau of Economic Research in Cambridge revealed that the sons of former Civil War–era prisoners of war were far more likely to die untimely deaths than the sons of soldiers who were not imprisoned, even though each subset of offspring was born after the conclusion of the war and, therefore, bore no direct impact of the imprisonment.[1]

For more than a dozen years we've known, as a result of studies conducted by top researchers, what our DNA looks like through microscopes, but now we've found a way to influence that DNA at will. It's called hormesis (or hormetic stress), which describes a phenomenon in which a substance or environmental agent known to be harmful in larger doses has stimulating and beneficial effects on living organisms when the quantity of the harmful substance is small. Living cells actually adapt in response to these substances (or stressors), positively affecting their condition and functionality.[2] This is something we can do consciously and, as a result, alter the structure of our primordial cells with specific intent.

Dr. Pierre Capel is a professor emeritus of experimental immunology at Utrecht University in the Netherlands. His research into DNA, cell structures, and the biochemical relationship between DNA and disease have served to greatly further our scientific understanding of how our bodies respond and adapt to environmental stressors. After reviewing and analyzing the results of our experiments at Radboud University, Dr. Capel validated my claim that we were the first to prove direct, conscious influence over the autonomic nervous system, the cell, our DNA, and gene expressions. Gene expressions, which refer to the process by which the instructions in our DNA are converted into a functional product, such as a protein, were previously believed to be involuntary. But once we began exerting influence over the autonomic nervous system — as we demonstrated at Radboud and Wayne State — we showed that a sequence of chemical processes could result in different, unexpectedly positive gene expressions. We showed that it was possible to suppress a negative reaction to a harmful toxin and to control the immune system. It may also be possible that we can influence our gene expressions by positively activating transcription factors (which convert DNA to RNA) and other proteins that cannot otherwise be influenced. If that is shown to be true, we will have the ability to positively direct transcription factors, which have hundreds if not thousands of potential gene expressions.

Naturally, this was a revelation to researchers like Dr. Capel and, I should hope, the larger scientific community. Because if we can consciously influence gene expressions in the present, we could potentially influence the expression of genes passed down to us through the DNA of our ancestors. That may seem farfetched, but the applications of that influence, in terms of disease prevention (think genetic markers) and treatment, not to mention other hereditary factors, are limitless. More research is necessary, of course, and we still have a great deal to learn about how to do this ethically and responsibly, but if we are able to alter that which has been transcribed through the DNA of previous generations, we can change our genetic destiny.

Here in the Netherlands, there's an old saying which, in essence, translates to "I bless your seven past generations and the seven to come." In America, there's the Seventh Generation Principle, which is based on a Native American philosophy that states that the decisions we make in the present result in a sustainable world seven generations into the future.[3] Well, we have technology now that enables us to analyze our DNA and look back as far as eleven generations to track its journey as it has manifested in our genes and their various expressions.[4] This technology is being used and analyzed now in a variety of interesting ways, with implications ranging from anthropology to economics, but in my opinion, none are more interesting than the way it informs our understanding of genetics. We can apply this technology to potentially end that which has been negatively stored up in our genes and to reclaim the light and spirit extinguished in past generations, channeling them into a new medium—a new body—that's you!

When we alter our DNA for the better, the genes we pass along to future generations become an ancestral gift instead of a burden. And by getting rid of what is negative, we also reach back and release those who came before us from whatever pain, trauma, or disease they themselves inherited and passed along, and bless them. The Native peoples—our ancestors—they knew. We came with our Western, colonial minds, dismissing the people living peacefully in harmony with nature as stupid, primitive. We took their land and tried to crush their spirit, out of a false sense of superiority. But now it's time for us to reconnect with the Earth and become native ourselves. And in doing so, we have the knowledge and technology to make amends with the spirits of the past, here and now. It's time to awaken to our true nature, which is one of liberation. We can make *that* our ancestral gift.

I believe it is possible to get back to the original cell condition from 3.77 billion years ago. The original cell was thriving, and that cell still exists right now in your body, in all living things. The energy of the dinosaurs, of all extinct animals, hasn't gone from this world; it has just changed its form. Those cellular building blocks are present within our bodies, and we are able to restore them to their original shape 3.77 billion years later. It's almost inconceivable, but we are now able to look through microscopes and see that the cell, the primordial cell, was being protected by proteins known among molecular biologists as "chaperones." These cells required protection because they are believed to have been "born" in highly acidic, very hot waters. The protective proteins enabled the cells to withstand these extreme conditions. We live today in a climate-controlled bubble of comfort in which our cells are no longer stimulated by cold, heat, or pressure anymore. Those dangers persist outside of our bubbles, of course, but because we rarely engage with them anymore, the chaperone proteins protecting our cells don't work like they once did.

I believe that with this method, we have discovered a way to restore these proteins and with them the original condition of the cell, reversing the consequences of genetic wrongdoing and freeing our bodies, minds, and souls from generations of unnatural conditioning, which have led us down a path toward disease, depression, and disharmony with nature. It's nothing abstract. We can free the spirits of the past. We can liberate ourselves and, in doing so, free the spirits of our ancestors from their own genetic burden. I'm sure that sounds like some hippie bullshit, but it's based in science. Our ancestors were right.

Centuries of colonization, exploitation, pollution, and insensitivity have taken their toll on mankind's collective consciousness, but we still need to be in harmony with nature if we are to achieve true happiness and health in this or any lifetime. We are just now awakening to what's written into our genes and how we can edit the code. It is my hope that with future studies we will potentially show that we are able to restore the original cell and its condition in pure energy, the cell as a physical entity that receives light, that receives the soul. Sounds farfetched, doesn't it? I admit that it does. But it's *your* soul, *your* light. What are you going to do with it?

You'd better get on this horse because it's running, and it's faster than you. The science will have to catch up to us, but we'll have all the evidence soon. As I said, science can sometimes move as slowly as a slow turtle, but it doesn't take a geneticist to see the possibilities here. Who are you? What are you? You can claim the power of your own mind, claim your destiny. What are you going to do?

Professor Capel has been at the leading edge of DNA research for more than forty years. He's an authority in the field, and his latest book, *Het Emotionele DNA* (*The Emotional DNA*) seeks to combine the magical world of feelings with molecular biology to explain how feelings direct our health and how we can influence them consciously.[5] Feelings, Dr. Capel argues, don't exist. They emerge. But where do they come from? Our DNA can be a carrier of old emotions, even those of past generations, because we inherit the genes of our ancestors. Sometimes those old emotions knock at our conscious door, asking, "Can you free me?" The Native people are in tune with this. They know that old spirits visit us in this way, through our emotions. Skeptics, naturally, dismiss this kind of awareness as nonsense, as some hippie bullshit, but they're wrong. I see experiences like these all the time in real people's lives.

One of them is Michel Sardon. We were in Poland, at the camp where I host my winter retreats. Michel is a tall, handsome man, a carpenter and teacher of carpentry who was very much connected with his mother, who had died. He's a big, strong guy, but emotionally he was very much repressed. After a couple days of training, he went with our group up Mount Śnieżka, as has become our custom. We were nearing the ridge atop the mountain that marks the border between Poland and the Czech Republic, and there was a lot of wind. And it just got to him. He's a strong, handsome man who's always in control — he's a teacher and all — but the wind just broke him. I call it "the whip" because it beats the shit out of you, and that's exactly what it did to Michel. He was shaking uncontrollably, and I had to take him to an old customs control house over the border and hug him for a half hour to bring him back. Eventually we went back down the mountain together, and as we neared the bottom, he said, "I was talking to my mother all the way down."

Michel was a free man, a happy man. We played football later that day. But that moment on the mountain, overwhelmed by these trapped emotions and the force of the elements, was not only about his experiences in this lifetime or about his mother. It was also about the ancestors trapped within his genetic code, his DNA. His conditioned mind, like so many, wasn't able to tap into the depth of those mechanisms, which is why the experience overwhelmed him emotionally. Collectively, we have lost the native ability to bring harmony, emotionally and spiritually, into the here and now. But what is the purpose of life? Is it for your self-actualization alone? Or do you also carry the burden of responsibility to free the spirits of those who are locked up within your genetic code, like a safe. As long as we are alive, we are capable of getting to the safe and deciphering the combination.

But how seriously should we take the influence of emotions on our health and in our lives? Emotions can sometimes be difficult to process or understand. The people who attend our retreats often report that they see faces while doing the group breathing, faces they don't recognize but that they nevertheless feel a deep connection with. These visions, while mysterious, are vivid. Three-dimensional. And I argue that they are manifestations of our emotions and the condition of our physicality. These encrypted, deep genetic expressions come to life in our consciousness when we dive deeper into our ourselves, and we are able to free them when they do. And afterward, you feel much better because you have unburdened yourself of this genetic debt. You feel lighter. It's not abracadabra, it's genetics. It's science. You dial in the combination, open the safe, and free all the spirits that have been locked away within your DNA. Generations and generations. It's incredible.

Michel is a prime example, but he is just one example. For instance, I was in Barcelona recently, and after the group breathing session, a crying man approached me and said, "You gave me back my soul." What would you do if someone said something like that to you? These people come to me crying. They're beautiful people, but they're repressed emotionally. The breathing opens them up. They go deep within themselves and surrender to the emotion, crying like babies. The feelings overwhelm them. I just hug them and say, "Be strong and pass it on because there are more spirits confined within you and you can free them. Now you know how."

This is an exciting time. Through new developments in technology, researchers are gaining a better understanding not only of how they can manipulate DNA sequences but also how they can produce functionally relevant changes to the genome through epigenetics, which does not involve altering the DNA sequence but instead expression of the gene.

This research is at the center of Dr. Elissa Epel's work as the director of the Aging, Metabolism, and Emotion Center at the University of California at San Francisco. Dr. Epel, who with Nobel Prize–winner Dr. Elizabeth Blackburn, her former UCSF colleague, cowrote the *New York Times* bestseller *The Telomere Effect* in 2017. The John W. Brick Mental Health Foundation is funding a two-year gold-standard study, led by Dr. Epel, in which Dr. Epel's team will seek to determine how the body responds, on a cellular level, to hormetic stress as it relates to depression and mental health.

In the study, Epel is monitoring three groups: a control group that does nothing, a high-intensity interval training (HIIT) group, and a group that practices the Wim Hof Method. Naturally, having a researcher of Dr. Epel's stature investigating the efficacy of the method is an honor, and my hope is that her findings will grant further legitimacy to our claims. We know that the method does wonders for those suffering from depression and other mental health issues because we see it every day, but having a preeminent researcher validate what we see can only help to strengthen our case.

WHM AND BIPOLAR DISORDER

Despite having a very secure upbringing and loving family around, I never felt confident or safe on the inside. I was always scared and had difficulties adapting to changes in life. School was harsh, both theoretically and socially. Later in life, I could never keep a job, and I thought (and was told) it was because I was lazy and had poor character. I struggled with this reality for many years, never fitting into daily life or modern society.

At the age of forty-two, I had come to the road's end. I didn't see a way out of the darkness. I had been battling bipolar disorder for over thirty years, and life was really tough. So, when I found Wim, I literally fell to the floor crying because after three decades, I had finally found the tools to mend myself.

Wim showed me a flicker of light in my darkness, and I grabbed onto it like my life depended on it.

By applying this method into my life, I was able to break free from isolation, depression, pain, and fear. Through breathing exercises and cold exposure, I've been able to create space between depression and mania. That space has given me the time to find myself. Exterior triggers and negativity have no permanent hold over me anymore because I am more in control of my own emotions. Step by step, in collaboration with my doctors, I've removed almost all the medication I had been taking for so long for my mental disorder, and now I'm learning more and more to become my own healer by being more open and conscious in life.

The Wim Hof Method is for me personally the purest way back to who I really am, and by walking this road, I've been able to grow strong from the inside out, no longer looking so much to others but rather trusting myself.

ANDREAS GUSTAFSSON
STOCKHOLM, SWEDEN

But why does the method work so well to clear our ancestral trauma? As we discussed earlier in this chapter, inflammation influences the transcription factors, which directly relate to the expression of genes within our DNA. Through the method, we are now not only able to suppress inflammation but to activate the chaperone proteins that protect the cell, ensuring that undesired gene expressions do not occur. With that, the telomerases and telomeres (proteins that protect the ends of chromosomes from damage) that influence the length and quality of our lives, keep the cells going. We are therefore able to influence our health spans (the number of years we remain healthy, active, and disease-free) and the quality of our gene expressions, and set in motion a chain of reactions that positively influences our health on a cellular level.

If we are able to influence the expression of our genes and eliminate undesired genetic outcomes that affected past generations negatively, we can look at those outcomes the same way a psychotherapist helps one to look at trauma. As. Dr. Capel has argued, emotions are tied up in our DNA, which makes them heritable. And just as we are unable to address emotional trauma in the moment, it is only with the perspective afforded by distance that we are able to address our emotional inheritance. Once we remove ourselves from the immediacy of our trauma and can view it from an observational distance, we come to understand in psychotherapy that we are not responsible for the abuse we have suffered, the trauma that has been inflicted upon us that has affected us so deeply. It is only then that we are able to heal.

Similarly, when we examine and analyze the expressions of our genes throughout the generations (again, we now have the technology to reach back eleven generations), we can edit the physical structure of our DNA and free it of its own hereditary trauma here in the present. The key, as with psychotherapy, is distance. We do not indulge or compound the trauma but instead address it from a clinical remove, a vantage point from which emotion does not factor. Because the trauma is in the past, it does not manifest as anxiety. And we can restore our genes on a cellular level to their original condition, 3.77 billion years ago, before environmental and biological factors corrupted their expression in the form of disease, depression, and other abnormalities locked up within our DNA. We can free ourselves and future generations of that burden.

Are you following me?

Allow me to take it a step further. When we first go into the cold water, it's a shock to our system. Our body reacts in an extreme way, activating the survival instinct — the fight, flight, food, freeze, and fuck response — as it seeks to protect itself from this harsh environmental stimulus. But once the mind and body, working in concert, begin to acclimate to this new, extreme environment, they neutralize the magnitude of the cold's impact. And if we go into cold water on a regular basis, our vascular system gradually changes as a result, which means more blood flow into the deeper part of the brain, into the periaqueductal gray hemisphere, converting the pain associated with the initial shock into a pleasurable sensation.

We are able to survive and move on from traumatic gene expressions in a similar way. Trauma, like the cold water, is beyond our immediate control. We feel its impact, our survival mechanisms are activated, and we lock it away. Later, we deal with its consequences. Or we don't, and they stay locked away. Your parents, grandparents, or great-grandparents may not have been able to deal with their trauma, but they passed it along through their genes. Now we are able to cleanse our genes from that trauma and start anew, freeing all those generations. Their freedom is the conduit to our own as reflected by the soul. It's up to us to translate its energy. The soul emits light, electricity. If you are able to go into the deepest part of the brain, you come into connection with it. And you will know when it happens because the feeling is unmistakable. Trauma's got nothing on the soul.

BREATHING FOR MOOD REGULATION

This exercise uses and trains neurostimulative brain control to help alleviate moodiness or depression. Supplying oxygen to the brain improves a person's well-being. We have seen in fMRIs that the whole brain dances when subjects do the breathing exercises. You can do this exercise whenever you feel like it, but it can be an especially powerful exercise to try if you are feeling melancholy, moody, or depressed. Do not force it — feel it!

1 Sit or lie down in a safe, comfortable place.
2 Feel and try to relax every part of your body. Observe and be aware of what you are feeling, seeing, and hearing, without judgment. Just be present.
3 Take twenty deep breaths. Fully in and letting go.
4 On the last breath, breathe in deeply, hold it, press your chin toward your chest, tense your pelvic floor, and direct that tension up your core toward your head.
5 If you are experiencing any physical discomfort, focus your attention there and observe. Tense the muscles in that area. Hold the breath for a maximum of ten seconds.
6 Release the breath and all tension.
7 Repeat two or three times or until you feel better.

You don't need to be an advanced practitioner of the method to get there. If you do the breathing and open your heart to the experience, you can forge this connection in twenty minutes. That's one of the most beautiful things about the method. Anybody who does it is able to get into the deepest part of their brain and free whatever is locked up in their body, like blockages, fears, inhibitions, whatever is interfering with their energy flow. We are here on this physical plane as a result of all the generations that came before us, and we are able to free them as well because we carry them with us in our genes, like an inheritance or, in the case of trauma, a burden. No more. We are each equipped with the tools to free ourselves, physically and psychologically, from all of this cumulative trauma, and now is the time to get it done. We are able not only to ensure our happiness, strength, and health, but also ensure the same for future generations to come. We're standing at the threshold.

Because the soul is eternal, there is no beginning and no end, no time or space. There is only the soul, infinite and beyond our comprehension, yet absolutely present and guiding us back toward nature, toward our true selves. And because there is no beginning or end, there is no death. The soul transcends the body, transcends all matter. In the brief time that we occupy our body, we can seek to reach an understanding of the light within that defines our existence, and that is how we come to access the multitudes, to paraphrase Whitman, contained within us. We don't have to accept the world the way it is if it doesn't respect the soul.

This is the way I have always felt, even before I went into the cold water. I don't know what it is exactly, but I'm not going to accept all this disease and war, hungry children, cruelty to animals. I'm not going to accept any of it. Exploitation, insensitivity, is that the goal of humanity? Is this what we are teaching our children in school? To participate in a system that serves greed and ignorance? The hell with that. No. To make sense of the world, we must return to nature. That's why I am exploring extremes with my body and mind, going back to science. I'm showing that there's another way. There's a whole range of natural solutions to the contemporary problems we are facing. There's a way out.

I'm here because of the light. It has guided me on a mission to reveal the true nature of humanity, which is love. It's time to wake up to that love. It's time to awaken to a mind that is not vulnerable to manipulation or corruption, that is 100 percent yours. How do you achieve that? By breathing, going into the cold, becoming conscious, reflecting the soul. We get there by being the light.

I don't mean this in some sort of abstract sense. There's a logic to it. There is science. It is through the light of the soul that we will find our purpose and sense in this crazy world. This is what I have been doing for forty years now, but in many ways, I feel as if my journey is only beginning. I just want to go straight to the existential crux of it all and show that if we change the paradigm—if we make the case for a return to nature—we are able not only to ensure our happiness, strength, and health, but also ensure the same for future generations to come.

What else do you want?

12

BEYOND THE FIVE SENSES

We are each born with the innate capacity to tackle disease, both mentally and physically. We are built to be alert, present, and in control, but modern mankind has become alienated from its true nature by dwelling on thoughts, worries, and stress, which manifest in the body as inflammation. We think we've got the world around us controlled, but the reality is quite the opposite. Our comfort-zone behaviorism has made us weak. More than that, it's made us dependent. We sit in 72-degree rooms and watch television while eating processed "comfort" foods to escape from the self-imposed stresses of our daily lives. And while it's nice to contemplate, to go and space out with your thoughts from time to time, we've become vessels of deregulation. Our immune systems have become compromised, leading to disease and disorder. Our biochemistry is out of balance, and we can no longer function as we were meant to. On top of that, much of this illness is psychosomatic. We are worrying ourselves sick.

Through the method, we've now found a way to return to our natural state of being. We've discovered a way to hop off the hamster wheel and reconnect with the nature within ourselves. As a guinea pig of sorts, I have developed and refined the method by putting it to extreme tests: going up Mount Everest in shorts, swimming beneath the ice, hanging by one finger, running a marathon in the desert without drinking. I did all of that to show that I could not only survive but maintain control, even in the most extreme environments and conditions. That's nature, mine and yours.

We are each a divine being within, right here in this moment. The light is here within you as you hold this book in your hands. If you can be present in this moment instead of dwelling on worry and stress, you can set yourself on a course toward happiness, strength, and health. Those are the properties of the light within if you are able to recognize it. But if you can't (or won't) and instead allow negative thoughts and energy to direct you, you will only become further alienated and disconnected from that light. And when we lose connection in that way, we fail to harness its power.

These breathing techniques and gradual cold exposure are so effective that they allow us to go even into the unseen. Because we have senses that are going outward and we have senses that are going inward. And the unseen senses are now within our reach, as are the deepest parts of the brain. That might sound very spacey and very out there, but it isn't. There's nothing abstract about it. It's physics, it's biochemistry, and it's your will, which is a neurological muscle. We're learning how to enter into our own minds.

This is where the three pillars of the method come together. The breathing, cold exposure, and commitment aren't as powerful individually as they are together. But if you are able to connect with your body through the breathing and cold exposure—if you commit to and train in the method—then suddenly this neurological muscle called "will" is able to enter and to do its beautiful work. The will is your enthusiasm and energy for life. That's the power of your beautiful mind. It becomes beautiful because you are in command. Where would you like to go?

Until now, the consensus scientific opinion has been that we are not able to tap into our subconscious minds. We could perhaps catch a glimpse in our dreams or, perhaps, through some tarot cards or astrology. But just as consciousness requires a neurological awakening and development—a child gaining first awareness of itself and, in time, learning to walk, for example—so does the subconscious need to be awakened. And when the subconscious is awakened and developed, it becomes conscious. While the scientific research on this is somewhat recent, it's important to bear in mind that this isn't a new or radical concept. Much to the contrary, the merging of the conscious and subconscious mind is a practice that goes back thousands of years, a sort of spiritual heritage. Cultures throughout time have created practices or rites of passage that seek to connect to a truer sense of reality, the sense of the soul. What is the soul? It is the "you" beyond thinking. It is nature itself.

Perhaps you have experienced flashes of strange insights, moments of deep clarity. Or maybe you have sensed an energy within yourself that you couldn't quite identify. That's your subconscious knocking on your consciousness's door. It's part of who and what you are. To connect with it, you first have to learn how to deal with your body. Then your mind. From there you get into your spiritual body, and then finally, you get to know your subconscious and seek to answer life's big questions: Why am I here? What is my purpose? And if your neurological muscle is sufficiently developed, all of your faculties should be ready to serve you. You will possess the ability to walk with your spirit consciously. Your subconscious becomes aware, the unseen becomes seeable, and you at last encounter and, in time, gain control over your senses—all of them.

Did you know that in addition to your five external senses—smell, sight, taste, hearing, and touch—you also have other senses? Science recognizes a number of extra senses such as proprioception and interoception. And though the prevailing thought has been that we cannot control these internal senses, the Wayne State study showed that it is possible to have top-down control over them.

People think of the sixth sense as "extrasensory perception," like reading minds or telling the future. But I call the sixth sense "confidence," the absolute confidence in your own nature, your own destiny, your mission, your purpose on this earth and beyond. This is an extraordinarily powerful sense that transcends doubt and allows for no confusion. Instead, it's pure light. It shines within you. When you have confidence in it, you have the power to go and follow its path.

It's like the old story from the Hindu epic, the *Mahabharata*, in which five brothers are gathered for an archery lesson. The master instructor ties a wooden fish high up on a tree above a body of water and asks each student, one by one, to assume their archer's stance and to take aim at the fish's eye while looking only at its reflection in the water. As each brother steps forward to take his shot, the instructor stops him and asks, "What do you see?"

"The sky, the tree, the water . . . ," the eldest brother says before the instructor cuts him off.

"The branch of the tree, the fish . . . ," the next oldest says before meeting the same fate.

When it's the youngest brother's turn, he answers, without hesitation, "I see the eye of the fish."

"Shoot!" says the instructor. And the young archer shoots his arrow right through the eye of the fish.

The moral of the story is that when we focus on the eye of the fish instead of allowing ourselves to be distracted by the branches and the water, we gain the confidence to take action. That is the same confidence you will feel when your subconscious comes to your awareness. It's the same confidence that propels me toward my mission and that enables me to see it and pursue it with clarity. You will be drawn in, too, because, like the youngest brother, you cannot miss. There's only one shot to take. Take it and in doing so discover the purpose of your life. Let the light guide you, and go with confidence.

Proprioception (or kinesthesia) refers to an awareness of one's body position and movement through space. Proprioception is mediated by proprioceptors, which are mechanosensory neurons located within muscles, tendons, and joints. These neurons form an electrical network throughout the body that enables us to connect with our sense of balance, reflexes, and other bodily functions. By learning new body movements like yoga, juggling, dancing, or even climbing, you can develop these senses even more. This is what I have been doing all my life, practicing yoga, gaining more focus and body awareness, getting in better tune with my body, learning to trust my body's intelligence.

Another sense I want to talk about is interoception, which can be broadly defined as an awareness of what's going on within our bodies. Interoception is what tells us when we are hungry or full, hot or cold, or when we need to use the bathroom. There is even evidence that it might just be that infamous "sixth sense," the "gut feeling" we know we should follow.[1] Just as there are proprioceptors in our muscles and joints that detect movement, so, too, are there receptors in our internal organs, including our skin, that signal their functionality to the brain. It was also long believed that this sense, interoception, was beyond our conscious control. But we are able to influence it. Our minds can go anywhere in our bodies, become aware of what is happening there, and influence it.

Here's what I have observed. Over time, cold exposure and the breathing practice brings you to a more sensitive state. You are then able to detect subtle internal processes. The interoceptive practice of focusing on the heartbeat at the end of this chapter is a great way to develop this. I have shown that I am able to ignite the release of hormones and maintain my skin temperature despite exposure to cold water. I did this with my mind, with the power of intention. Trust in your own ability—confidence—combined with alertness puts the body and mind in a state of heightened awareness. That heightened awareness, or interoceptive focus, translates to top-down control over these supposedly involuntary systems. But it's the power of the mind *itself*, not of thoughts or thinking. When you learn to still the mind, you get to the point where you can internally activate neural activity. It is a shift that goes from external awareness, to stillness, to internal awareness, to the self beyond thinking. After you have set your mind, you trust. This power lies past the thinking brain. Again, it is a feeling, not a thought. And if I can suppress an adverse reaction to the stress of cold water on my skin, just think of the broader applications. Stress, of course, exists in many forms, but if we can resist bacteria, viruses, daily stress, emotional trauma, what have you, we can get in there and neutralize those biochemical consequences. Yes. Do you see?

INTEROCEPTION WITH THE BREATH

How would you like to train your sense of interoception and sharpen your interoceptive focus? If you are already practicing the Basic Breathing Exercise, you are on your way. This visualization practice will take you to the next level.

1. Sit or lie down in a safe, comfortable space and close your eyes.
2. Breathe normally, but focus on your breathing. Fully in and letting go.
3. Now consciously take a deep breath in through the nose, and exhale through the mouth. Do not force it.
4. Visualize your lungs, and consciously feel the oxygen entering your lungs. Interoception is now beginning.
5. Take some more deep breaths. In through the nose, out through the mouth. Nice and easy.
6. After a few more breaths, visualize the exchange of gases in your body. Visualize the oxygen going from the lungs, through the capillaries and into the blood, and visualize the excretion of carbon dioxide upon exhalation.
7. If you notice that your mind has started to wander, simply reset your focus to your breath. Over time, you will learn to become more mindful and gain more control over your mind and be less consumed by your thoughts.
8. Practice this exercise for several minutes.

In a 2018 cover story for *Scientific American*, neuroscientist Dr. Jonathan Kipnis of the University of Virginia School of Medicine wrote that "mounting evidence indicates that the brain and the immune system interact routinely, both in sickness and in health."[2] That same year, writing in the *Journal of Experimental Medicine*, Dr. Kipnis wrote that he "would like to propose that the defining role of the immune system is to sense the microorganisms and to deliver the necessary information about them to the brain." The immune response, therefore, should be hardwired in our brain, which makes the immune system, according to Kipnis, also a sense.[3] In the endotoxin study, practicing the method enabled us to suppress a reaction to an injection of a harmful bacteria, thus activating the innate immune response. We could therefore say that we have conscious influence over this sense.

Anyone who awakens their extra senses by practicing the method is capable of consciously igniting and activating the body's ability to fend off illness, making it more resilient. The ability is there within us all. It's ours. Just do the breathing and the gradual cold exposure and see for yourself what it does for your physical and mental health.

Do the breathing. Breath is the life-force, and it will enable you to prime your biochemistry so that when stress occurs, you are ready to deal with it. Now you are like a gardener tending to his or her garden, which is your body. When storms come, or animals break through the fence, or people drive over it, you are able to restore your garden with the power of your interoceptive focus. That's the power of the mind at work. Whatever is going on in any part of your garden, you are able to go there and restore that which has been negatively influenced and biochemically knocked out of balance, causing a collapse called disease. Amazing, eh?

This is a beautiful thing, because now more people will understand that we are built to be in control within, at will, more than we previously thought was possible. We have to restore this awareness, the subconscious coming to our consciousness, if we are to heal ourselves and maintain biochemical balance and harmony in the depths of ourselves. We can each be the gardener of the beautiful flowers of life every single day. I welcome further scientific inquiries and investigations into these ideas, especially among the skeptical, because I know that they will only serve to polish the diamond of the truth. I know in my heart that we are on the right path. This is my mission, as set into clear focus by my own sense of confidence.

I want the diamond of the truth to be polished so that everybody can see how beautiful it is, how accessible, how powerful and effective it is. We can control our minds and our bodies. We can sense what is happening within us and change it. We will win this war caused by the inner terrorists of bacteria, viruses, distress, oxidative stress, emotions. Whatever form the stress takes, you are able to tackle it and restore health, happiness, and strength to your body because you are one with the soul, the life-force. And the life-force is good. It's goodness itself. There we are. And we are one.

The mother in Baghdad is the same as the mother in New York or the mother in Beijing. They all wish the same for their children, which is that they grow up to be happy, strong, and healthy. That's the greatest gift you can give to a child, or to anyone, because what else is there?

So let's get back to the core values of life that we are born with and tend to our gardens in peace. Let's not invest ourselves in hopelessness but instead in positivity, in being present, in the conviction that we are the commanders of our fate and the captains of our soul. Once you become happy, strong, and healthy, you radiate like the sun, and you pass your warmth onto others. You become a healer, and there is divinity in that healing that transcends language and the dogma of our societal conditioning. We are here to share the love with the mothers in Baghdad, New York, Beijing, and any other place in this world. We are here to give peace, strength, happiness, and health to all of our children, because that is what they deserve. See the fish's eye and shoot, my friends.

I guarantee that you will not miss.

INTEROCEPTION OF THE HEARTBEAT

In this exercise we are going to forge a conscious connection with the heart and circulatory system. Because the heartbeat is involuntary, few of us pay much attention to it or to the circulatory system it serves. But if we channel our interoceptive focus to it, we can decrease our heart rate during times of stress, which not only serves to relieve that stress but also to improve the absorption of oxygen and nutrients within our cells. Here's how:

1 Sit or lie down in a safe, comfortable space.
2 Relax.
3 Feel and visualize your heartbeat.
4 Connect with your heartbeat and try to synchronize your breath with it so that you can feel it everywhere.
5 Now visualize your circulatory system. Visualize that with every inhalation, oxygen-rich blood is flowing from your lungs to your heart, to every part in your body, through a network of blood vessels that could wrap around the earth two and a half times. Imagine how your blood provides oxygen and nutrients to organs and muscles, and transports waste products (like carbon dioxide) to your liver, kidneys, and lungs.

6 Reconnect with your heartbeat and try to synchronize your breath with it again.

7 Make a journey through your body and try to feel the heartbeat in different parts of it. If you focus on your hand, feel the heartbeat there, and if you focus on your feet, feel the blood flow from your ankles to your toes.

This is connecting your mind and your body. This is interoceptive focus. A couple of minutes per day is enough to help you deepen this connection and reap the benefits of it.

13 INTO THE LIGHT WITHIN

My method is effective, but I don't want people to think of it as some sort of doctrine or me as some sort of guru. Doctrines and gurus are for those still battling with the ego, while science — the truth of things — has no use for ego. Solid scientific data isn't speculative. It's real whether you believe it or not. With the method, I struck upon a fundamental truth. If you do A, then B comes, and from B, C, and then D. It's simplified, easy to understand, and the results can be seen and felt more or less immediately. I searched for that deeper truth for years. I had read hundreds of books. But when I went into nature and encountered the merciless but righteous cold, it brought me into that depth of understanding instantly. Instead of reading about it, I experienced it through an understanding beyond language that stilled my mind. And then the cold taught me the deeper breathing. I became an alchemist, and I found that I could do unimaginable things.

At first I hid what I had discovered from everybody because I was afraid of their judgment. I imagined them ridiculing me for going into the cold water that way, calling me a crazy man, a fool. When I finally mounted the courage to reveal myself, that is, of course, exactly what happened. They all called me a madman and mocked me. To be sure, many still do. And you know what? They're right. I'm crazy about life, I am! I love it! How do you feel when you're in love? You're crazy about somebody. You feel crazy! Well, I'm crazy about life. And how come? Because I go beyond. I'm literally out of my mind. I exist in the whole of my body. I make myself feel good, strong, and healthy, and I'm able to maintain that feeling. And now, through my seminars, courses, and this book, I have the platform to show the world how they can feel that way too. We can all be mad together.

The purpose of this book is to bring various new insights to light and to change the way we perceive consciousness, human potential, and the truth of nature so that we can all experience happiness, strength, and health. We can express this knowledge to those we love, but our genes also express it, benefiting our descendants. It's a perfect circle that perpetuates itself through love. It's representative of the cycle of life. A flower blooms, and then it dies, but no, it lives on when the next flower rises. As Walt Whitman wrote more than 150 years ago in "Song of Myself," "the smallest sprout shows there is really no death." He was right then, and he's right now. The energy just goes on and on and is never lost.

The flower is a symbol. It doesn't die; it just changes its form. The same is true of us. Our energy returns to the earth, but our knowledge, our consciousness remains. That's the beauty. The method itself cannot answer the mystical questions of the universe for you—*Why are we here? What is the purpose of life?*—but it reflects a truth through which you can find the answers within yourself. Not everyone has the same purpose in life or the same goals, but the method can help bring them into focus. It certainly did for me.

Going into the cold forged, from my earliest explorations, a great spiritual awareness. I'd go into the cold water, but I wouldn't feel cold. Instead, in the stillness of the freezing cold water, I found a kind of connection to something greater. It's all about connection. Do you know what the word "yoga" means? Yoga means connection; it comes from the verb *yug*, and *yug* is "to connect." This is what the author of *The Yoga Sutras of Patanjali* wrote sixteen hundred years ago or so, more or less. It still holds. "Yoga is silencing the modifications of the mind, then the seer dwells in his own nature," Patanjali wrote in Sutras

1.2 and 1.3.[1] But who is the seer? The seer is the witness, the pure consciousness. If you understand that sentence, you don't have to read all the thousands of sutras that follow it. But if you don't understand that sentence, you're fucked. You'll have to follow all the pathways of yoga, learn about the *chakras*, the *kleshas*, the *chitta vritti*, just like I did. All of those things, man. None of the spiritual texts I had were in my native language, but I read them. I learned Sanskrit. I was always crazy about learning languages and was searching for the real mysticism behind the real yoga. I sought out a teacher at a Hindu temple in Amsterdam. Even though I didn't have any money to pay him, he liked that I wanted to learn. My goal was to read all of the Yoga Sutras and the Bhagavad Gita. I went through all of it, and I still couldn't understand shit. It was all intellectual. But in an instant, all those years ago, the cold taught me to silence my thoughts. I began to breathe, deeply and automatically. This brought me to the power of the nervous system, to that pure consciousness, to the light within.

According to science, we have no control over our autonomic nervous system—the deepest part of our nervous system. But I challenged that belief. I also challenged the belief that you have to practice yoga for decades to have such control over your body. We showed at Radboud that after just four days of training in the mountains and six days of solo practice at home, the autonomic nervous system could not only be influenced, but accessed deeply and activated. We did that through the breathing techniques, through breath retention. In Sanskrit, the retention breaths are called *kumbhakas*: *bahya kumbhaka* for the exhale and *antarik kumbhaka* for the inhale. *The Yoga Sutras of Patanjali* is a great work, but like the Bible, it's largely impenetrable due to its antiquated language. It makes a lot more sense to me than the Bible or the Quran do, though, because it's not about subjective orientations, moral codes, or dogma. It just shows you the way the body and the mind work. Yoga is a universal technique, and it still makes sense today. Our understanding of it just needs to be updated.

That's what we are doing. We have updated it all through the scrutiny of scientific research, so there is no speculation about it. The method is well-fitted to serve and soothe the neurology of our mind, of our contemporary spirits and their experience. When I was younger and went seeking a deeper truth, I read the works of all the great yogis past and present, from Patanjali up through Krishnamurti and Osho. In reading Yogananda, I discovered tales of the legendary immortal Babaji, and as I continued to search, I later encountered the works of Thomas Merton, Alan Watts, Gurdjieff, Ouspensky, and many more extraordinary philosophers and thinkers. But despite absorbing all that knowledge and acknowledging its enduring wisdom, I simply could not get it straight within my own spirit and within my own mind. There was something missing that I couldn't quite identify until I encountered it in nature and in the science that helped me to understand what I was feeling.

I have been on this path for forty years, but it's only really been the past twelve years in which the scientific community has begun to come around to these ideas by demonstrating their validity in laboratory studies. Some will surely continue to dismiss me and scoff at what we are doing, but that's their problem, not mine. We're showing it. This isn't speculative. Like Patanjali wrote, I have become the seer, and I dwell in my own nature. I believe what I see. I look to the future of humanity and know with profound certainty that we can change it. We are going to show that the soul and the love and the power and the strength and the health and the happiness are ours and that all the rest is bullshit. Because it is. Go past your conditioning and realize that this is what you were born to be: 100 percent alive, aware, and in control of your mind and your body. This is the secret to our collective enlightenment. *Tat tvam asi.* There's a little more mystical Sanskrit for you: "That way thou art."

There is a wealth of knowledge to be found in ancient texts across cultures. And by all means, dive deep. It is a beautiful journey, to immerse yourself in the pursuit of knowledge. But don't get caught in the mind. We have learned so much unnecessary data and endured so much wrongheaded, indoctrinating schooling that we have been deprived of our human birthright of well-being. Instead, many of us serve a system that is polluting, exploitative, and insensitive. But we don't have to live that way. It's time that we wake up to our senses, to our common sense of love, of protecting each other, and live in harmony with nature. Keep it simple and remember that feeling is true understanding.

I'm serious. Look, I'm a person who used to host tree-climbing birthday parties for neighborhood children. As a boy, I played Tarzan in the forests near my hometown. I explored Western Europe by bicycle and the canyons of Spain with ropes tied around my waist. I pondered and philosophized. I read a ton of books, but I was searching for something else, a feeling. And then I went into the water. That was my peace, my solace. There was connection — boom — it was there. I felt it. You could call it spirituality or transcendence or whatever else you like, but for me it was more about how it felt. It didn't need a word because I knew what it was.

Each of us is guided by an inner voice, or a feeling like the one I just described, a voiceless guidance deep within us. Sometimes, amid all the noise and stress and daily worries — bills and mortgages, children and relationships, work and schedules, politics and religion — it can be difficult to connect with this voice, but it's there, hardwired into our neurology. It's always been there, and it will show us the way if we let it. Yet we have been indoctrinated into believing that we have to solve our problems through our thoughts, through the induction and scrutiny of questions and answers, of ideas, when all we really have to do is listen to what nature is telling us. To what our true nature is telling us.

The modern world is like an infinity symbol or Möbius strip, a looping racetrack that goes on endlessly, and it's not good for us because we can't get off the horse. Hell, man, we *are* the horse. But deep down we just want to *be*. Without the noise of outside voices, without the distractions of life. Just being and feeling contentment in the stillness of it, our blood flowing into the deepest parts of our brain — our primitive mammalian brain — like a child who has yet to acquire language, just feeling, sensing. Like being in love. While your conscious mind is seemingly ever-present, love activates the deeper parts of your brain and enables you not to think but to fly, to feel vulnerably. To give yourself over to the power it wields, however illogical it appears because, as they say, the heart wants what it wants. Don't I know it.

BREATHING FOR STRESS CONTROL

Stress is the killer in our Western society — all that thinking, going into overdrive, making deadlines. They really are dead lines! Stress deregulates our system. You can tell if you are stressed by counting how many times you breathe in a minute. Try it now with a timer. If you're breathing between fifteen to twenty times a minute, you are stressed.

What I do for stress is one minute of humming and breathing. This always works for me. It taps into your parasympathetic nervous system — where the peace is inside — and calms down your hectic sympathetic nervous system. And it's like a massage for your spine from within — all the way up to your brain stem and to the center of your head. It brings you directly inside your body.

1 Set a timer for one minute.
2 Settle yourself somewhere comfortable.
3 Breathe in deeply.
4 Breathe out with a sound like "Hum," "Ah," or "Om." Make whatever sounds make you happy.
5 When you run out of air, breathe in deeply and let it out with another "Hum."
6 Continue until the timer stops.

How many times did you breathe in a minute of humming? Maybe four, five, six times? Nice.

I wrote back in chapter 3 about how the modern human brain experiences significantly less blood flow into its deeper parts than the brains of our prehistoric ancestors. Yet if we can consciously direct our blood flow into those deeper parts, into the limbic system (which, again, governs memory and emotion), into the brain stem and the periaqueductal gray hemisphere, our brains would not only survive, but bloom, as if watering a flower. It would be like the desert after the rains come. Suddenly, within a few days, it's all colors. The seeds of life were there all along. How, then, to bring that rainwater, that blood flow, into that part of your brain where you feel and experience the world beyond the mental racetrack? The eternal world. How do we get off the horse?

I'll tell you what I do. I follow my inner voice and listen to what it tells me. I trust my soul sense and let it guide me. I ignore, as best as I can, my ego. I know it's going to be cold in the morning and that those first few seconds in the cold water are going to be unpleasant because my ego tells me so. But my inner voice tells me to bloody get into that cold water because it is calling me to embrace every bit of my being. It tells me it's healthy and the right thing to do, while my ego continues to argue the opposite, even after all these years. It's like the proverbial angel and devil sitting on my shoulders, whispering into my ears, and I'm caught in between. The key is being able to tell which one is the angel and which one is the devil. Most people can't make this distinction, or they don't want to, because the truth is uncomfortable. They don't want to step off the racetrack because they have found comfort in its predictable contours. They'd rather intellectualize than feel because feeling makes them vulnerable. They can't control the outcome. They can't explain it with words.

But me, I don't even acknowledge the racetrack. I'm a wild horse. Unbroken. I follow my inner voice, the same voice that first led me into the cold waters of Beatrixpark all those years ago. Every day I follow it back into the water, and I know it's good. Once I get in, the noble nature of the cold gets at me with all the might of the earth and becomes a tender touch, very intimate. I know I'm going to get something like three or four times more energy after doing it. Because when I go into the cold, the deepest parts of my brain, like the brain stem, which governs the survival instinct, receive blood flow. And that turns on the rest of my body. It's like an activation. And when I get out of the water, I feel alive, as if I have experienced a rebirth.

The human body is well-equipped to endure gradual exposure to ice water. The water offers us a way to handle stress, mental or physical, of any kind. It can be painful at first, but you learn to adjust to it and then, eventually, you actually start to love it. You start to love that stress and what it does for you. Hormetic stress in this form is exhilarating and beneficial. And it helps to protect the body, on a cellular level, from other stressors, whatever they might be. Bacteria, viruses, emotional stress, work stress. Anxiety heightened by congestion, sitting there every day, unable to deal with that stress, becoming annoyed.

If you go into the cold water with regularity and gradually increase your exposure, protective mechanisms in your body and mind will activate and alleviate the stress. Of course, follow the protocols as outlined in chapter 3: thirty seconds, forty-five seconds . . . you understand. You build up to a minute in the cold, then two, et cetera. Once you get past the initial shock and calm down, the stress falls away. There are no tyrannical bosses or heartbreaking divorces in the ice bath. The cold water is the boss.

The cold leads the way toward a spirituality of the mind, a calmness with which you can handle any other stress. It is a spirituality that exists beyond the ego and maintains the soul. And it's strong. That's what I found on Mount Everest when I was lost in a whiteout in my shorts. There was nobody else around, it was freezing cold, and there was little oxygen. But despite all of that, I remained calm. I felt no stress, and that was my mind. I was past the "death zone" on the highest mountain in the world in nothing but my shorts, losing my way, and I couldn't see anything anymore. My left foot was frostbitten. I wasn't scared. I wasn't anxious. I gained control. In a moment in which everything was seemingly out of control, my mind took control, through the breath.

You don't have to climb past the death zone to feel out of control though. Life can be full of tumult and uncertainty. We've developed the ability to launch rockets and people to the moon, but we're not able to maintain our own happiness, strength, and health? How poor we truly are. How little we control.

Are you in command? Are you living up to the light in your soul? Are you making sense to yourself? No? Well, the spiritual state of your mind is right here. The soul too. Breathe. Relax into the cold. Get the blood and electricity flowing. Feel it. Understand beyond words. Know. The spirit is inside of you. Just open up to it and direct its light to others. That's love.

I say no ego. We go. We connect with each other through love and sharing. This spirituality is inherent in us and our innate neurological pathways, but somehow we lost our ability to find it, like the people in the story in which the wise men decide where to put the soul. Before I die, I want to prove through science that it actually is quite easy to see and feel the presence of your soul, to see and feel and realize the purpose of it all. It's where East, the way of the heart, and the West, the way of the mind, come together. But not only East and West, but North and South, Above and Below. That's the crossroads of the cosmos, the *bindu*, where all creation begins, where we reside within the universe. But whatever the symbols, we move beyond religion and instead rely on science to show the way. If you want to achieve spirituality, then find the way of the light. We have the tools to get into that now, to cleanse ourselves, and to learn to control and to direct the light within. Toward what? Toward *moksha*, liberation, *samadhi*, the prima, liberty. Awakening to the flow of our subtle energy, *ki*, *qi*, *prana*. It's all there for you if you want to be free.

But what is freedom for you? How much freedom is enough freedom? Are you okay with maybe, you know, only being free on the weekends? Do you have time for freedom?

The power of the mind is incredible. It has top-down command over your body and all of the senses. It is able to command the seen and the unseen, the visible and invisible. We're not just mammals with some thoughts. We have consciousness, the natural tendency to transcend the ego into something more. That's why we are here. Spiritual systems across the world recognize a subtle energy within us, the electricity that flows up and down the spine and throughout the body.[2] Balancing this flow and tapping into its power is the purpose of practices like yoga and qi gong. But it's your decision how far you go. Do you want peace in your mind? Breathe it alive and take away the stress. Do you want to enter into the most mystical of traditions and gather their fruits? Forget studying difficult languages and going into a cave for twenty years. Just breathe on the sofa in the morning before breakfast.

Inspiration means to breathe in. *Inspire*. Spirit. Life. People get hung up on getting the breathing right. They think it is too simple to work. They ask me, "How do you do it, Wim? Is it with the nose, or the mouth? Do I fill the belly, the diaphragm? Or do you have to close

The breath and the cold take you to the depths of yourself

one nostril and then the other? Do I fill the lungs all the way, or not too much, or . . ." And I say, "It doesn't matter what kind of hole you use here, just get it in!" Go easy. Don't think so hard about these things, just get the breath in. Into the belly, the chest, and the head—and let it go. Keep it simple. Some people are so in their head that they have to relearn how to feel, to train their interoceptive sense of their internal experience. That's why we say that beginners should start breathing through the nose, so they don't go over the limits of the body. The body wants nutrients, oxygen, and vitamins, and it wants light. The breath ignites our inner electricity. It connects our consciousness with nature, with all that is. That is liberation, and we can do it consciously. Isn't that amazing? You can do it with just twenty minutes of breathing. Within the time span of twenty minutes, you can experience timelessness and understand eternity. Just being with the light consciously, any stress is gone. You transcend your thoughts. There is no doubt anymore. You become everything. It's right here, right now.

I know from my experience that the breathing method provides an effective means to cleanse all our emotional trauma, blockages, inhibitions, and fears. As I said in chapter 4, if you do Wim Hof breathing in a group setting, the experience is intensified. Humanity was birthed into the tribe. We are still tribal. The simple act of breathing together allows the emotions to come to the surface faster. It is this simplicity itself that allows space for a nonjudgmental state of mind that beckons a shared vulnerability. When I work with groups, I can feel their reluctance to allow the emotions to come up, but when the energy builds, it creates a domino effect: one person cries, another laughs, someone else screams, and it is all okay in that moment, the moment that is held by the group.

The breathing alone is a transformational technique that has the potential to change mental health care because it endows the practitioner with a sense of control of what is rightly theirs: control of their mind and their heart, opening up to feed the brain with love and power that is not to be repressed. These breathing techniques are so simple and so effective that all you have to do to reclaim your genetic destiny is push the button. That's your mind. At first you cleanse yourself with the breath and the cold, alkalizing your body and reducing inflammation. You condition your blood flow to go deep into the brain. Then you can use the breath and the power of the mind to cleanse your past emotions and your trauma. Those are the *chitta vrittis* (distracting thoughts) and the *kleshas* (poisonous emotions) in the old yoga. You cleanse them with the prana (energy) that flows through your chakras (energy centers) that run from the base of your spine and up to the top of your head along three parallel channels called the *ida*, *pingala*, and *sushumna*.[3] And on and on. With the method we have demystified all this and brought it up to date, helping to bring the science of yoga into the modern age.

UNITE WITH THE LIGHT: THE "STROBOSCOPE" EXERCISE

Beautiful being, beautiful soul, would you like to illuminate your consciousness? Come, just lie here on the sofa. Are you comfortable?

Do you feel good? Hey, what did you do this morning? You say you woke up?
I did the same thing! Wow, parallel universe. You say you have stress,
tension, all that mental shit? Whatever you are thinking, I don't care. Let
it go. Let it go. Now all there is for you to do is relax and breathe. Just drop
everything and get into this breathing. We are all lightworkers. Work with the
light and get free.

1 Sit in a relaxed, comfortable position.
2 Close your eyes, follow your breath, witness yourself calming down.
3 Just look at what you see with your eyes closed. Don't try to see anything
   in particular. Be patient. In this way, your energy is able to disconnect from
   the external perception of the visual cortex and go into the deeper realms
   of the brain.
4 Keep following your breath, and turn your inner focus to the center of your
   forehead, the "third eye." You may see a luminous halo that pulses with your
   breath — in, out, in, out, like the flashing light from a stroboscope. You might
   feel you want to look more directly at it, but then you will take away the
   intensity. Learn to let it be. This is a phenomenal way to subtly observe the
   neural activity of your brain.

Once you have some experience with this meditation, try adding the focus
on the center of your forehead to the Basic Breathing Exercise. You may start
to have spontaneous experiences of your inner light.

EPILOGUE

HOW TO CHANGE THE WORLD

We have been led by directors and presidents and kings and queens for a long time, but the crowns belong to us. We are all kings and queens, and we should behave like it. We should be proud. Your kingdom, of course, is you, yourself. There's no castle. *You* are the castle. The universe is contained within you, and you are capable of doing extraordinary things.

This is nature's call to the moment, where past and present converge in the depths of our being to show us a way forward. What do you think? How do you feel? Are you excited to explore deeply within yourself, gain awareness, and take control? Why? What do you want to do with that power? What will you do with the abundance awaiting you within?

To be in control of that emotion called life, in the purest way, you must experience it through the lens of love. Love will open you up to the power of your mind, and suddenly you find yourself standing before the abyss of your experience, sensing a soul you did not think was accessible, let alone controllable, as if it were some sort of abstract thing. Consumed by the reality and stress of daily life, you entertained no such notions. Yeah, maybe on a Saturday you'd sit and ponder a little bit with a nice glass of wine, contemplating philosophy and whatever's going on in the world, but by Monday morning, you're up and off to work again, and the stress begins anew. But I'm here to tell you it doesn't have to be that way. The real spirit, the real experience of your mind and your body is one of happiness, strength, and health. The method enables you to gain control of what is an unlimited mind, which opens your conscious eye and brings the light where it belongs, right here, right now, in all its splendor. That's who you are. That's how you will find not only peace, but bliss. Yes, the breath is a door. But love welcomes you inside.

Critics and skeptics will, of course, say that I've got my head in the clouds, that I should be practical, that I should just shut up already. But how can I be quiet when I'm dwelling in the seat of the mind? I'm sending these signals into the hemispheres, into the ethereal world, into the past. The expression of the soul transcends our concepts of time and space. It's right here, right now. The past, present, and future are one, and you can access them like going into a library and picking out the right book. You can make use of this library at any time because it's yours. It was always yours. It is your birthright to be happy, strong, and healthy. Your destiny is yours, my friends, and you can find it in the breath.

In the natural course of practicing the method, you will, in time, see light. You will be attracted to its energy. And if you follow the flow of that energy with conviction and with love, you can bypass and transcend all of the scriptures and their repressive dogmas. You can exist outside of time. You can explore all the parts of your brain, free the spirits of the past, cleanse your DNA, and within the uninterrupted flow of your own neurology, cast away the darkness for good. You are the witness, the seer, as Patanjali wrote nearly two thousand years ago. You can silence the modifications of the conscious mind and dwell within your own nature. So, what are you waiting for?

Our minds are like dogs that have been tied to a tree. Or like children who have been told to sit still and be quiet. These restrictions work in opposition to our nature. Dogs need to run free just as children need the freedom to play and explore. The same is true of our minds. When we release our minds from the bondage of dogma, the stress of daily existence, and our perceived limits, we can glimpse a new world where love and harmony with nature prevail. Evolution has made us into the humans we are, yet after two hundred thousand years, humankind has yet to find its place in the natural order. That's why we live in a world marked by war, poverty, hunger, disease, and suffering. We're so busy trying to survive that we have lost sight of our own consciousness. We have stepped out of the light, purposefully, and into chaos. It's not sustainable.

But now the time has come for us to reclaim what we have lost, to harness the consciousness, and to direct it back toward the light and rediscover the soul. This can be our revolution. Our purpose can be to spread love and happiness far and wide, bring peace through conscious action, and return to a state of harmony with the nature from which we have evolved. That nature is within us and always has been contained in the DNA of the first living cell. This is how we will change the world, one soul at a time, altering the collective consciousness by awakening to our own boundless potential. We are limited only by the depth of our imagination and the strength of our conviction.

Is it really that simple? Yes. We are now standing at the threshold of this greater understanding. Our minds will take us on a journey toward true self-actualization in which we will convert the subconscious into the conscious and the soul into light. It may take us a while, but that's us. That's what we were meant to be. Can you see it? Can you feel it? If you can't, or if you're afraid of what you might find (or fail to find) within you, just place your faith in the method. Take a cold shower. Do the breathing. Activate your vascular system. Change your biochemistry. Follow the breath. Lean into it. The breath goes everywhere, and it will lead you where you need to go.

Let go of your ego and instead reflect that which connects us, which is love. Let go of your thoughts and your stress and open up to your heart. It is only when you let go that you will truly be able to reconnect with the universe, with the nature buried deep within your cells. Let go and allow your soul to rise in your consciousness. The soul is eternal, indestructible, and perhaps most importantly, incorruptible.

Let go and become the king or queen you were meant to be. I know you can do it. I believe in you.

ACKNOWLEDGMENTS

This book has been a universe unto itself. So many beautiful figures have played their role. The diamond of the depths, distilled into a book, carefully polished, finally shown.

To Tami Simon, of Sounds True, who recognized the space people need to go deep and, consequently, made it possible to get the depth to the people.

To producer Mitchell Clute, for his talent of receiving, like a bed for a river's flow—a true natural power. Editor Mark Weinstein, who channeled the flow into powerful segments, nourishing the soil with crystal clear intent. Jennifer Yvette Brown, who wandered around the labyrinth of words and turned stones into flowers, opening up the eyes of everybody who worked on the book, giving light touches to heavy matters. Erin, who knows me better than I know myself, who brought in new life and gave depth to the book through meticulous scrutiny. My son Enahm, with his protective wings; my daughter Isa, with her tender yet determined touch. Everyone at the Hoffice and at Sounds True. All of you have worked on this with the patience of monks in a monastery—sacred the energy. My gratitude goes to all of you.

Not to mention all of the dedicated professors and doctors behind the groundbreaking studies and insights: Dr. Ken Kamler, Dr. Peter Pickkers, Dr. Matthijs Kox, Dr. Maria Hopman, Dr. Geert Buijze, Dr. Vaibhav Diwadkar, Dr. Otto Muzik, and many more. Their work has led to an absolute new horizon of what humans are capable of. They are seekers, helping bring that which is hidden into the light. And there is more to come. I trust my gut feeling to know more than my consciousness is able to see. That is exactly what I want to show in this book, that which is unseen, yet so strong.

To Dr. Elissa Epel, who delighted my heart by writing the foreword of this book. A brilliant scientist and an absolute shining light who is bringing the Wim Hof Method into a new realm.

To the Wim Hof Method community—from the bottom of my heart, I thank you. I thank you not only for your support, but for sharing the soul. You are the soul of this movement. You are the heart. All the people I have met over the years, all the stories—it makes me smile to think of it. We meet in love.

And to you, my dear reader, I acknowledge you. It is time to go home, to where we recognize our true being together. Happiness, strength, and health are the moral values of our being, and they are back.

Last but not least, to Zina, my brown shadow, my dog, my guru. She embodies loyalty, warmth, unconditional love, and selflessness. In the mountains, she is three times faster than any of us. She only wants care. I only want care. I care for you. We care for each other.

No doubt, this is only the beginning.

FAQS

GENERAL

How much time do I need to invest to see results from this method?
The average daily investment is twenty minutes at the start of your day. See the WHM At-A-Glance: Three Pillars of a Daily Practice guide on page 72. Build up to the full practice at your own pace and find your own way to apply the method in your daily life, naturally integrating the exercises in this book into your exercise or meditation regimen. For example, you can focus on deeper, more conscious breathing any time during the day. The method should be implemented in your life daily to reap the full benefits.

Can the WHM help with my health condition?
Since the Wim Hof Method moderates the immune response, it is most effective with conditions that arise from an underlying disturbance to the immune system. However, positive results have been observed with a wide variety of conditions. Although the Wim Hof Method has been credited with bringing symptoms into complete remission in some cases, WHM practices should be seen as tools to help manage your health, rather than as a cure.

There has been considerable scientific research into the Wim Hof Method and its effects on various health conditions. The results are very promising, and there are more research findings to come. There are, however, hundreds of thousands of conditions and diseases. For the majority of ailments, we do not have the requisite knowledge to be able to speak with authority on the potential of the WHM as an effective treatment. Note also that results vary greatly from person to person due to personal and physiological differences. Ultimately, the best—and really the only—way to find out what the Wim Hof Method does for you personally is to give it a try. Some conditions may be negatively impacted by WHM practice. If you have a chronic health condition or are currently ill, consult with a medical professional before implementing the Wim Hof Method.

Is this method for everybody?
The Wim Hof Method can be practiced by every healthy individual. Listen to your body and never force the practices.

We advise against practicing the WHM if you are dealing with any of the following:
- Epilepsy
- High blood pressure (Particularly if you are taking a prescription medication)
- Coronary heart disease (e.g., Angina Pectoris; Stable Angina)
- A history of serious health issues like heart failure or stroke
- If you suffer from migraines, we urge you to be cautious about taking ice baths.

Can I practice the WHM when I am pregnant?
Out of precaution, we also advise against WHM practice if you are pregnant. We do not know if the changes in biochemistry associated with the WHM techniques adversely affect the health of the baby. When the baby is born, you are safe to resume practicing the Method.

Is the WHM suitable for children?
Many families enjoy practicing the WHM method together. Children's brains are still developing, however, and they are not equipped with the self-regulation necessary to assess any risks associated with the method. Thus, we advise that children under the age of sixteen are supervised by a parent or legal guardian, and are never compelled to practice the method against their will. Please be careful with regard to cold exposure, and build this up gradually.

COLD

I really hate the cold. Do I really have to do the cold showers?

If you want to receive the benefits of the method, yes. Staying in our "comfort zone" weakens our system and ends up hurting us in the end. But take it gradually. Enjoy your warm shower thoroughly, and increase your cold exposure time at the end only as you are ready. There should be no force involved in this process.

What if I stay cold after the cold shower?

First, reduce the time you spend in the cold shower. Start with just 15 seconds and increase the time gradually to adapt yourself to cold exposure, just as you would work up to a more strenuous workout. Your body will soon begin to warm up faster after cold exposure sessions.

You can also use the mindset practices in this book to program yourself both before and after your cold shower, using the power of the mind to remain in control of your body's responses and to maintain your motivation.

Lastly, doing the horse stance exercise when you get out of the shower will heat you up from the inside out and help you keep your focus.

I live in an environment where the showers are not that cold. What should I do?

Check the temperature of your cold tap water. The health benefits of the method start at 60 degrees Fahrenheit, so it is likely that your cold water is just cold enough. You can experiment with extending your exposure time a bit if your water temperature falls in this zone.

Is there any proven benefit to switching back and forth between hot and cold showers?

Cold exposure boosts the release of norepinephrine, a neurotransmitter involved in focus, attention, and mood. Norepinephrine also acts as a hormone, promoting vasoconstriction and thus decreasing the total surface area by which heat is lost to its surroundings. The greater the jump in temperature, the more norepinephrine is released. It therefore follows that going from hot to cold repeatedly could augment the benefits received from this neurotransmitter. The effect is thought to be more pronounced with more extreme swings, such as alternating between ice bath and sauna. Although alternating between hot and cold exposure is a time-honored practice in many cultures, research on it is lacking, and conclusive findings have yet to be established.

BREATHING

How many times a day do I have to do the Basic Breathing exercise?
We recommend the standard three to four rounds in the morning before breakfast as a regular practice. Try a round in the mid-afternoon if your energy starts to wane.

How important is it to increase my breath retention time?
Extended retention time is not necessary to receive the health benefits of the method. If you lose consciousness from holding your breath out, you are taking the practice too far. Inhale once you feel the urge to do so. Listen to your body, not the ego!

Is it necessary to take the cold shower directly after the Basic Breathing exercises?
No, but doing the breathing practice first can help with your mind-set and cold tolerance. If you are not able to shower directly after, you can do a mini breathing exercise before you step into the cold shower — thirty deep breaths while focusing on your intention.

My fingers tighten up during the breathing exercises — what is happening?
You may experience involuntary muscle contraction, known as "tetany." Intensified breathing causes an efflux of CO_2, which in turn starts a cascade of ionization changes that leads to increased sensitivity of nerve cells. These then require less excitation to engender a muscle response, to the point where muscles can contract spontaneously. The effects are typically expressed most distinctly in the hands and feet, but can extend across the entire body.

Barring any preexisting medical conditions, this phenomenon is entirely harmless, and the effects dissipate within minutes. Over time, it may no longer arise at all. If the sensation is painful, please consult a medical professional.

My ears are ringing after the breathing practice — is this normal?
This effect is known as "tinnitus," a condition with a wide range of causes and manifestations.

For some people, practicing the WHM either induces or exacerbates the ringing, while for others it changes the pitch. Conversely, those dealing with chronic tinnitus often find relief from its concomitant anxiety in the calming effect of the breathing techniques.

The connection between tinnitus and the Wim Hof Method has various possible causes. Medical research shows a direct link between pulsatile tinnitus and anemia, which the WHM may ameliorate through the elevated oxygen intake. The breathing exercises also increase neural activity in the auditory brainstem, where the brain processes sounds, possibly causing auditory nerve cells to become over-excited.

The scientific community continues to grapple with the particulars of tinnitus, but has established that the phenomenon itself is harmless. We have found that in the vast majority of cases, the ringing disappears with repeated breathing practice. If you find that, after several weeks, the noise persists or intensifies, some underlying physiological condition may be at play, in which case we recommend you consult a medical professional.

NOTES

FOREWORD: AN UNLIKELY MEETING

1. G. A. Buijze, H. M. Y. De Jong, M. Kox, M. G. van de Sande, D. Van Schaardenburg, R. M. Van Vugt, C. D. Popa, P. Pickkers, and D. L. P. Baeten, "An Add-On Training Program Involving Breathing Exercises, Cold Exposure, and Meditation Attenuates Inflammation and Disease Activity in Axial Spondyloarthritis—A Proof of Concept Trial," *PLOS ONE* 14, no. 12 (December 2, 2019): e0225749, doi:10.1371/journal.pone.0225749.

2. M. Kox, L. T. van Eijk, J. Zwaag, J. van den Wildenberg, F. C. G. J. Sweep, J. G. van der Hoeven, and P. Pickkers, "Voluntary Activation of the Sympathetic Nervous System and Attenuation of the Innate Immune Response in Humans," *Proceedings of the National Academy of Sciences of the United States of America* 111, no. 20 (May 20, 2014): 7379–7384, doi: 10.1073/pnas.1322174111.

3. H. van Middendorp, M. Kox, P. Pickkers, and A. M. W. Evers, "The Role of Outcome Expectancies for a Training Program Consisting of Meditation, Breathing Exercises, and Cold Exposure on the Response to Endotoxin Administration: A Proof-of-Principle Study," *Clinical Rheumatology* 35, no. 4 (2016): 1081–1085, doi: 10.1007/s10067-015-3009-8.

PREFACE: IT'S ALL THERE FOR YOU

1. Mayo Clinic, "Multiple Sclerosis," mayoclinic.org/diseases-conditions/multiple -sclerosis/symptoms-causes/syc-20350269; Centers for Disease Control and Protection, "Lyme Disease," cdc.gov/lyme/index.html.

CHAPTER 1: THE MISSIONARY

1. Edgar Rice Burrows, "The Tarzan Series," edgarriceburroughs.com /series-profiles/the-tarzan-series/.

2. Jean M. Justad, "Hypothermia," State of Montana Department of Health and Human Services (2015), dphhs.mt.gov/Portals/85/dsd/documents/DDP /MedicalDirector/Hypothermia.pdf.

3. National Organization for Rare Diseases, "Weil Syndrome," rarediseases.org
    /rare-diseases/weil-syndrome/#targetText=Weil%20syndrome%2C%20a%20
    rare%20infectious,Leptospira%20bacteria%20known%20as%20leptospirosis.

CHAPTER 2: THE BIRTH OF THE ICEMAN

1. Dutch Amsterdam, "Squatting in Amsterdam," dutchamsterdam.nl/555
    -squatting-in-amsterdam.

2. Alesia Hsiao, "6 Amazing Benefits of Cold-Water Swimming," lifehack.org
    /288238/6-amazing-health-benefits-cold-water-swimming.

CHAPTER 3: A COLD SHOWER A DAY KEEPS THE DOCTOR AWAY

1. Joseph Castro, "11 Surprising Facts about the Circulatory System," *Live
    Science* (September 25, 2013), livescience.com/39925-circulatory-system-facts
    -surprising.html.

2. World Health Organization, "The Top 10 Causes of Death" (May 24, 2018),
    who.int/news-room/fact-sheets/detail/the-top-10-causes-of-death.

3. Castro, "11 Surprising Facts about the Circulatory System."

4. Julie O'Connor, "Novel Study Is First to Demonstrate Brain Mechanisms
    That Give 'The Iceman' Unusual Resistance to Cold," Wayne State University
    (February 28, 2018), today.wayne.edu/news/2018/02/28/novel-study
    -is-first-to-demonstrate-brain-mechanisms-that-give-the-iceman-unusual
    -resistance-to-cold-6232.

5. Otto Muzik, Kaice T. Reilly, and Vaibhav A. Diwadkar, "'Brain Over Body'—
    A Study on the Willful Regulation of Autonomic Function During Cold
    Exposure," *NeuroImage* 172 (February 2018): 632–641, doi: 10.1016/j
    .neuroimage.2018.01.067.

6. Marc Dingman, "Know Your Brain: Periaqueductal Gray" (July 17, 2016),
    neuroscientificallychallenged.com/blog/know-your-brain-periaqueductal-gray.

7. Wim Hof Method, "What Can I Do About Cold Hands or Cold Feet?"
    (January 5, 2016), wimhofmethod.freshdesk.com/support/solutions
    /articles/5000631655-what-can-i-do-about-cold-hands-or-cold-feet-.

CHAPTER 4: BREATHE MOTHERF*CKER

1. Gabriel R. Fries, Consuelo Walss-Bass, Moises E. Bauer, and Antonio L.
    Teixeira, "Revisiting Inflammation in Bipolar Disorder," *Pharmacology
    Biochemistry and Behavior* 177 (February 2019): 12–19, doi: 10.1016/j
    .pbb.2018.12.006; Lisa M. Coussens and Zeno Werb, "Inflammation and
    Cancer," *Nature* 420, no. 6917 (December 2019): 860–867, doi: 10.1038
    /nature01322.

2. Yogapedia, "Sat-Chit-Anada," yogapedia.com/definition/5838/sat-chit-ananda.

3. "Wim Hof Breathing Tutorial by Wim Hof," YouTube (September 28, 2018),
    youtube.com/watch?v=nzCaZQqAs9I&feature=youtu.be.

4. Geert A. Buijze and Maria T. Hopman, "Controlled Hyperventilation After Training May Accelerate Altitude Acclimatization," *Wilderness and Environmental Medicine* 25, no. 4: 484–486, wemjournal.org/article/S1080 -6032(14)00116-1/abstract.

CHAPTER 5: THE POWER OF THE MIND

1. Wim Hof and Koen De Jong, *The Way of the Iceman* (St. Paul, MN: Dragon Door Publications, 2017); Frits Muskiet quote w/ translator.

2. Henriët van Middendorp, Matthijs Kox, Peter Pickkers, and Andrea W. M. Evers, "The Role of Outcome Expectancies for a Training Program Consisting of Meditation, Breathing Exercises, and Cold Exposure on the Response to Endotoxin Administration: A Proof-of-Principle Study," *Clinical Rheumatology* 35, no. 4 (2016): 1081–1085, doi: 10.1007/s10067-015-3009-8.

3. "Wim Hof Breaks World Record," YouTube (January 26, 2008), youtube.com /watch?v=CEbfXUTiD08.

4. Kenneth Kamler, personal communication, September 17, 2009, wimhofmethod .com/uploads/kcfinder/files/WHM_DataInfo%20Kamler.pdf.

5. Joseph Angier, "Iceman on Everest: 'It Was Easy,'" ABC News (April 14, 2009), abcnews.go.com/Health/story?id=4393377&page=1.

6. "Wim Hof the Iceman in Radboud Hospital Research Facility," YouTube (August 23, 2010), youtube.com/watch?v=aINSboYgr_g&feature=youtu.be.

7. Jan T. Groothuis, Thijis M. Eijsvogels, Ralph R. Schoten, Dick. H. J. Thijssen, and Maria T. E. Hopman, "Can Meditation Influence the Autonomic Nervous System? A Case Report of a Man Immersed in Crushed Ice for 80 Minutes," innerfire.nl/files/can-meditation-influence-ans-hopman.pdf.

8. Radboud University Nijmegen Medical Centre, "Research on 'Iceman' Wim Hoff Suggests It May Be Possible to Influence Autonomic Nervous System and Immune Response," *ScienceDaily* (April 22, 2011), sciencedaily .com/releases/2011/04/110422090203.htm.

9. The Nobel Prize, "The Nobel Prize in Physiology or Medicine 2019" (October 7, 2019), press release, nobelprize.org/prizes/medicine/2019/press-release/.

10. Matthijs Kox, Lucas T. van Eijk, Jelle Zwaag, Joanne van den Wildenberg, Fred C. G. J. Sweep, Johannes G. van der Hoeven, and Peter Pickkers, "Voluntary Activation of the Sympathetic Nervous System and Attenuation of the Innate Immune Response in Humans," *Proceedings of the National Academy of Sciences of the United States of America* 111, no. 20: 7379–7384, doi: 10.1073/pnas.1322174111.

11. Heidi Ledford, "Behavior Training Reduces Inflammation," *Nature News* (May 5, 2014), nature.com/news/behavioural-training-reduces-inflammation -1.15156; Kox et al., "Voluntary Activation of the Sympathetic Nervous System."

12. Anne Houtman, Megan Scudellari, and Cindy Malone, *Biology Now* (New York: W. W. Norton, 2018).

CHAPTER 6: OLAYA

1. Encyclopedia Britannica, "ETA: Basque Organization," britannica.com/topic/ETA.

CHAPTER 7: WHM FOR HEALTH

1. Mayo Clinic, "Crohn's Disease," mayoclinic.org/diseases-conditions/crohns -disease/symptoms-causes/syc-20353304.

2. Centers for Disease Control and Prevention, "Arthritis: National Statistics," cdc.gov/arthritis/data_statistics/national-statistics.html.

3. Mayo Clinic, "Arthritis," mayoclinic.org/diseases-conditions/arthritis /symptoms-causes/syc-20350772.

4. American Autoimmune Related Diseases Association, Inc., "Autoimmune Disease Statistics," aarda.org/news-information/statistics/.

5. Wim Hof Method, "Senior Health Beyond Wellness," wimhofmethod.com /senior-health-beyond-wellness.

6. Nevco Health Care Education, "The Wim Hof Method for Seniors," nevcoeducation.com/product/senior-health-beyond-wellness-the-exercises/.

7. Anna Chojnacka, "Community for the Uninitiated One," Ted Talk, youtube.com/watch?v=8wGmE9qCnic&feature=youtu.be.

CHAPTER 8: WHM FOR PERFORMANCE

1. "Adenosine Triphosphate," Science Direct, sciencedirect.com/topics /medicine-and-dentistry/adenosine-triphosphate.

2. Michael M. Cox and David L. Nelson, "Glycolysis, Gluconeogenesis, and the Pentose Phosphate Pathway," in *Lehninger Principles of Biochemistry*, 5th ed. (New York: W. H. Freeman, 2008), 527–568.

3. Cox and Nelson, "Glycolysis, Gluconeogenesis, and the Pentose Phosphate Pathway," 527–568.

4. Wilfried Ehrmann, "Intense Breathing and Control of Immune System" (October 18, 2015), wilfried-ehrmann-e.blogspot.com/2015/10/intensive -breathing-has-amazing-effects.html.

5. "Alistair Overeem Talks Wim Hof Method," YouTube (March 3, 2016), youtu.be/5h_3NVI20T4.

6. Jelle Zwaag, Rob ter Horst, Ivana Blaženovi´c, Daniel Stoessel, Jacqueline Ratter, Josephine M.Worseck, Nicolas Schauer, Rinke Stienstra, Mihai G. Netea, Dieter Jahn, Peter Pickkers, and Matthijs Kox, "Involvement of Lactate and Pyruvate in the Anti-Inflmmatory Effects Exerted by Voluntary Activation of the Sympathetic Nervous System," *Metabolites* 10, no. 4 (2020): 148, doi:10.3390/metabo10040148.

7. Tara Parker-Pope, "On Your Marks, Get Set, Measure Heart Health," *New York Times*, May 23, 2011, well.blogs.nytimes.com/2011/05/23/on-your-marks -get-set-measure-heart-health/.

8. "Talking about the Wim Hof Method on the Dr. Oz Show," YouTube (July 22, 2019), youtube.com/watch?v=dEeWhsc5ZJ0&feature=youtu.be.

9. Wim Hof Method, "Wim Hof New World Record! (3 Hours Horse Stance)," YouTube (February 4, 2019), youtube.com/watch?v=uV3Oj6EDJxk&feature =youtu.be.

CHAPTER 9: THE TRUTH IS ON OUR SIDE

1. W. D. van Marken Lichtenbeld, J. W. Vanhommeirg, N. M. Smudlers, J. M. Drossaerts, G. J. Kemerink, N. D. Bouvy, P. Schrauwen, and G. J. Teule, "Cold-Activated Brown Adipose Tissue in Healthy Men," *New England Journal of Medicine* 360, no. 15 (April 9, 2009): 1500–1508, ncbi.nlm.nih.gov /pubmed/19357405.

2. "The Role of Brown Adipose with Wim Hof," Innerfire, innerfire.nl /brown-adipose.

3. Maartin J. Vosselman, Guy H. E. J. Vijgen, Boris R. M. Kingma, Boudewijn Brans, and Wouter D. van Marken Lichtenbelt, "Frequent Extreme Cold Exposure and Brown Fat and Cold-Induced Thermogenesis: A Study in a Monozygotic Twin," *PLOS One* 9, no. 7 (July 11, 2014): e101653, journals.plos.org/plosone/article?id=10.1371/journal.pone.0101653.

4. Vosselman et al., "Frequent Extreme Cold Exposure."

5. Mayo Clinic, "Ankylosing Spondylitis," mayoclinic.org/diseases-conditions /ankylosing-spondylitis/symptoms-causes/syc-20354808.

6. Dominique Baeten, "Evidence-Based Mindset & Physical Therapy for Add-On Treatment of Active Axial Spondyloarthritis: Safety and Efficacy" (June 12, 2018), ichgcp.net/clinical-trials-registry/NCT02744014.

7. Mayo Clinic, "Endometriosis," mayoclinic.org/diseases-conditions /endometriosis/symptoms-causes/syc-20354656.

CHAPTER 10: A DAY IN THE LIFE OF THE ICEMAN

1. "A3 Ballon Stunt Met Willbord Frequin en 'Bikkel' Wim Hof," YouTube (May 31, 2007), youtube.com/watch?v=PcEvotOB9wA&feature=youtu.be&t=185.

CHAPTER 11: FREEING OUR ANCESTRAL BURDEN

1. Dora L. Costa, Noelle Yetter, and Heather DeSomer, "Intergenerational Transmission of Paternal Trauma Among US Civil War Ex-POWs," *Proceedings of the National Academy of Sciences of the United States of America* 115, no. 44 (October 30, 2018): 11215–11220, pnas.org/content/115/44/11215.

2. Mark P. Mattson, "Hormesis Defined," *Ageing Research Reviews* 7, no. 1 (January 2008): 1–7, doi: 10.1016/j.arr.2007.08.007.

3. Indigenous Corporate Training, Inc., "What is the Seventh Generation Principle?" (May 29, 2012), ictinc.ca/blog/seventh-generation-principle.

4. Nicole Wetsman, "What This Unprecedented 13-Million-Person Family Tree Reveals," *National Geographic* (March 1, 2018), nationalgeographic.com/news /2018/03/human-family-tree-genealogy-ancestry-dna-marriage-longevity-science/.

5. Pierre Capel, *The Emotional DNA: Feelings Don't Exist, They Emerge* (Amsterdam: K.pl Education, 2018); English translation by M. L. Leslie Pringle, 2019.

CHAPTER 12: BEYOND THE FIVE SENSES

1. Narayanan Kandasamy, Sarah N. Garfinkel, Lionel Page, Ben Hardy, Hugo D. Critchley, March Gurnell, and John M. Coats, "Interoceptive Ability Predicts Survival on a London Trading Floor," *Scientific Reports* 6, 32986 (2016), doi: 10.1038/srep32986, nature.com/articles/srep32986.

2. Jonathan Kipnis, "The Seventh Sense," *Scientific American* (August 2018), scientificamerican.com/article/the-seventh-sense/.

3. Jonathan Kipnis, "Immune System: The 'Seventh Sense,'" *Journal of Experimental Medicine* (January 2018), rupress.org/jem/article/215/2/397 /42541/Immune-system-The-seventh-sense-Immune-system-The.

CHAPTER 13: INTO THE LIGHT WITHIN

1. Sri Swami Satchidanada, *The Yoga Sutras of Patanjali* (Buckingham, VI: Integral Yoga Publications, 2012).

2. Cyndi Dale, *The Subtle Body* (Boulder, CO: Sounds True, 2009).

3. Andrea Ferretti, "A Beginner's Guide to the Chakras," *Yoga Journal* (July 29, 2014), yogajournal.com/practice/beginners-guide-chakras.

GLOSSARY

ACUTE MOUNTAIN SICKNESS (AMS) The negative health effect of high altitude, caused by rapid exposure to low amounts of oxygen at high elevation. Symptoms may include headaches, vomiting, tiredness, trouble sleeping, and dizziness.

ADENOSINE TRIPHOSPHATE (ATP) A complex organic chemical that provides energy to drive many processes in living cells, including muscle contraction, nerve impulse propagation, and chemical synthesis. Found in all forms of life, ATP is often referred to as the "molecular unit of currency" of intracellular energy transfer.

ADRENAL AXIS A complex set of interactions and feedback loops between the hypothalamus, pituitary, and adrenal glands. This system regulates the body's response to stress, immune function, energy expenditure, mood, emotions, and libido.

AEROBIC CAPACITY The measure of the heart and lungs' ability to deliver oxygen to the muscles.

AEROBIC DISSIMILATION Refers to oxygen's (or respiration's) role in the decomposition of organic compounds and the conversion of proteins, nucleic acids, fats, and carbohydrates into simple substances. Aerobic dissimilation plays a key role in the body's productionof ATP.

ALKALINITY A measure of the acid-neutralizing capacity of water. Practicing the Wim Hof Method increases the alkalinity of the blood, resulting in various health benefits.

ANKYLOSING SPONDYLITIS (AS) A type of arthritis in which there is a long-term inflammation of the joints of the spine.

AUTOIMMUNE DISEASE A condition in which your immune system mistakenly attacks your body.

AUTONOMIC NERVOUS SYSTEM (ANS) A control system that acts largely unconsciously and regulates bodily functions, such as the heart rate, digestion, respiratory rate, pupillary response, urination, and sexual arousal.

BIOCHEMICAL RESIDUE The undesirable by-products of a chemical reaction.

BIOCHEMISTRY The study of chemical processes within and relating to living organisms. Biochemical processes give rise to the complexity of life.

BROWN ADIPOSE TISSUE (BAT) A unique tissue that is able to convert chemical energy directly into heat when activated by the sympathetic nervous system. While initially believed to be of relevance only in human newborns and infants, research during recent years provided unequivocal evidence of active BAT in human adults.

CANNABINOIDS One of a class of diverse, external chemical compounds that acts on cannabinoid receptors, which are part of the endocannabinoid system found in cells that alter neurotransmitter release in the brain.

CARDIOVASCULAR DISEASE A class of diseases that affect the heart or blood vessels.

CHAKRA A Sanskrit word that translates to "wheel" or "disk" and refers to subtle energy centers within the human body, most commonly understood as located along the spine, through the neck, brow, and at the crown of the head.

CHAPERONES Proteins that assist the conformational folding or unfolding and the assembly or disassembly of other macromolecular structures.

CITRIC ACID CYCLE A series of chemical reactions used by all aerobic organisms to release stored energy through the oxidation of acetyl-CoA derived from carbohydrates, fats, and proteins into adenosine triphosphate (ATP) and carbon dioxide.

COMFORT-ZONE BEHAVIORISM A conditioned behavioral state in which we seek to minimize our uncertainty, scarcity, and vulnerability.

CONSCIOUS BREATHING An umbrella term for medical and therapeutic methods that improve the breathing function. Conscious breathing methods involve directing awareness to breathing and developing habits that improve respiration. Human respiration is controlled consciously or unconsciously.

CROHN'S DISEASE A type of inflammatory bowel disease (IBD) that may affect any segment of the gastrointestinal tract from the mouth to the anus. Symptoms often include abdominal pain, diarrhea, fever, and weight loss.

DEOXYRIBONUCLEIC ACID (DNA) A molecule composed of two chains that coil around each other to form a double helix carrying genetic instructions for the development, functioning, growth, and reproduction of all known organisms.

DIABETES A group of metabolic disorders characterized by a high blood sugar level over a prolonged period.

DIMETHYLTRYPTAMINE (DMT) An intense, naturally occurring psychedelic that's also found endogenously in the human body.

ENDOCANNABINOID Molecules produced naturally by cells in the human body that bind to and activate cannabinoid receptors.

ENDOCRINE SYSTEM The collection of glands that produce hormones that regulate metabolism, growth and development, tissue function, sexual function, reproduction, sleep, and mood, among other things.

ENDOMETRIOSIS A disorder in which tissue that normally lines the uterus grows outside of the uterus.

ENVIRONMENTAL STRESS Stress caused by stimuli in our environment, like war, temperature, noise, and crowds.

EPIGENETICS The study of how the expression of DNA can be changed without changing the structure of DNA itself.

FIGHT, FLIGHT, OR FREEZE RESPONSE A physiological reaction that occurs in response to a perceived harmful event, attack, or threat to survival.

GASP REFLEX An involuntary reflex caused by sudden immersion into water colder than 70 degrees Fahrenheit.

GENE EXPRESSION The process by which information from a gene is used in the synthesis of a functional gene product, such as a protein.

GLYCOPROTEIN A type of protein molecule that has had a carbohydrate attached to it.

HORMETIC STRESS (HORMESIS) A theoretical phenomenon in which something that produces harmful biological effects at moderate to high doses produces beneficial effects at low doses.

HYDROCARBON An organic compound (such as butane) containing only carbon and hydrogen and often occurring in petroleum, natural gas, and coal.

HYPERVENTILATION A condition in which you start to breathe very fast.

HYPOTHERMIA When the body loses heat faster than it can produce heat, causing a dangerously low body temperature.

HYPOXIA Deficiency in the amount of oxygen reaching the tissues.

IMMUNE SYSTEM A host defense system comprising many biological structures and processes within an organism that protects against disease.

INFLAMMATION A process by which the body's white blood cells and the substances they produce protect us from infection with foreign organisms, such as bacteria and viruses.

INTERCOSTAL MUSCLES Several groups of muscles that run between the ribs and help form and move the chest wall. The intercostal muscles are mainly involved in the mechanical aspect of breathing.

INTERLEUKIN Any of a class of glycoproteins produced by leukocytes for regulating immune responses.

INTEROCEPTION The sense of the internal state of the body. This can be both conscious and nonconscious.

LACTATE A salt or ester of lactic acid. Lactate is a product of fermentation and is produced during cellular respiration as glucose is broken down.

LACTATE THRESHOLD The lactate threshold is the maximal effort or intensity that an athlete can maintain for an extended period of time with little or no increase in lactate in the blood.

LEUKOCYTE A type of blood cell that is made in the bone marrow and found in the blood and lymph tissue. Leukocytes are part of the body's immune system and help the body fight infection and other diseases.

LIMBIC SYSTEM A complex system of nerves and networks in the brain, involving several areas near the edge of the cortex concerned with instinct and mood. It controls the basic emotions (fear, pleasure, anger) and drives (hunger, sex, dominance, care of offspring).

LIPIDS Molecules that contain hydrocarbons and make up the building blocks of the structure and function of living cells. Examples of lipids include fats, oils, waxes, certain vitamins, hormones, and most of the cell membrane that is not made up of protein.

LUPUS A long-term autoimmune disease in which the body's immune system becomes hyperactive and attacks normal, healthy tissue. Symptoms include inflammation, swelling, and damage to the joints, skin, kidneys, blood, heart, and lungs.

LYME DISEASE An infectious disease caused by the Borrelia bacterium, which is spread by ticks. Lyme disease causes a rash, often in a bull's-eye pattern, and flu-like symptoms. Joint pain and weakness in the limbs can also occur.

LYMPHATIC SYSTEM A network of tissues and organs that help rid the body of toxins, waste, and other unwanted materials. The primary function of the lymphatic system is to transport lymph, a fluid containing infection-fighting white blood cells, throughout the body. Part of the vascular system.

MAMMALIAN BRAIN The portion of the midbrain that is comprised of the limbic system, believed to be the control center for emotion and learning.

METABOLIC ACTIVITY The set of life-sustaining chemical reactions in organisms. The three main purposes of metabolic activity are the conversion of food to energy to run cellular processes; the conversion of food/fuel to building blocks for proteins, lipids, nucleic acids, and some carbohydrates; and the elimination of nitrogenous waste.

METABOLIC RATE The rate of energy expenditure per unit time by "warm-blooded" animals at rest.

MITOCHONDRIAL PROCESSES The processes through which mitochondria (cellular organelles) take in nutrients, break them down, and create energy-rich molecules for the cell.

MULTIPLE SCLEROSIS A potentially disabling disease of the brain and spinal cord in which the immune system attacks the protective sheath that covers nerve fibers and causes communication problems between your brain and the rest of your body.

MUSCULAR PLASTICITY   The ability of a given muscle to alter its structural and functional properties in accordance with the environmental conditions imposed on it.

NEUROLOGICAL PATHWAYS   A series of connected nerves along which electrical impulses travel in the body.

PARASYMPATHETIC NERVOUS SYSTEM (PNS)   One of three divisions of the autonomic nervous system, it conserves energy as it slows the heart rate, increases intestinal and gland activity, and relaxes sphincter muscles in the gastrointestinal tract.

PARKINSON'S DISEASE   A long-term degenerative disorder of the central nervous system that mainly affects the motor system.

PERIAQUEDUCTAL GRAY   An area of gray matter found in the midbrain that plays a critical role in autonomic function, motivated behavior, and behavioral responses to threatening stimuli. It is also the primary control center for pain modulation.

PHENOTYPE   The composite of an organism's observable characteristics or traits.

PINEAL GLAND   A small endocrine gland in the brain of most vertebrates that produces melatonin, a serotonin-derived hormone that modulates sleep patterns.

POLYMER   A compound of high molecular weight derived either by the addition or condensation of many smaller molecules.

PROPRIOCEPTION (KINESTHESIA)   The sense of self-movement and body position. It is sometimes described as the sixth or seventh sense.

REPTILIAN BRAIN   Another name for the basal ganglia, structures derived from the floor of the forebrain during development. The term derives from the idea that neuroanatomists once believed that the forebrains of reptiles and birds were dominated by these structures. The reptilian brain is believed to be responsible for species-typical instinctual behaviors involved in aggression, dominance, territoriality, and ritual displays.

RHEUMATOID ARTHRITIS   A long-term autoimmune disorder that primarily affects joints. It typically results in warm, swollen, stiff, and painful joints. Rheumatoid arthritis most commonly affects the wrist and hands.

RIBONUCLEIC ACID (RNA)   A polymeric molecule essential in various biological roles in coding, decoding, regulation, and expression of genes. RNA and DNA are nucleic acids, and, along with lipids, proteins and carbohydrates, constitute the four major macromolecules essential for all known forms of life.

RIBONUCLEOPROTEIN   A complex of ribonucleic acid and RNA-binding proteins. These complexes play an integral part in a number of important biological functions that include DNA replication, regulating gene expression, and regulating the metabolism of RNA.

SATCHITANANDA   A Sanskrit term that describes the nature of reality as it is conceptualized in Hindu and yogic philosophy.

SATURATION METER (OR PULSE OXIMETER)   A device that measures the oxygen saturation levels in one's blood.

SYMPATHETIC NERVOUS SYSTEM   Part of the autonomic nervous system (ANS), which also includes the parasympathetic nervous system (PNS). The sympathetic nervous system activates what is often termed the fight-or-flight response.

TELOMERASE   A ribonucleoprotein that adds a species-dependent telomere repeat sequence to the ends of telomeres and protects the end of the chromosome from DNA damage or from fusion with neighboring chromosomes.

TELOMERE   A region of repetitive nucleotide sequences at each end of a chromosome, which protects the end of the chromosome from deterioration or from fusion with neighboring chromosomes. Some researchers believe that a progressive loss of telomeres helps propel aging.

THERMOREGULATION   The ability of an organism to keep its body temperature within certain boundaries, even when the surrounding temperature is very different.

TRANSCRIPTION FACTOR   A protein that controls the rate of transcription of genetic information from DNA to messenger RNA by binding to a specific DNA sequence. The function of TFs is to regulate—turn on and off—genes in order to make sure that they are expressed in the right cell at the right time and in the right amount throughout the life of the cell and the organism.

TUMMO   An ancient technique of Tibetan Buddhism combining breathing and visualization to enter a deep state of meditation that is used to increase one's "inner fire."

TUMOR NECROSIS FACTOR A cell-signaling protein involved in systemic inflammation whose primary role is in the regulation of immune cells.

VAGUS NERVE The longest and most complex of the twelve pairs of cranial nerves that emanate from the brain. It transmits information to or from the surface of the brain to tissues and organs elsewhere in the body.

VASCULAR SYSTEM The system of vessels that permits blood to circulate and transport nutrients (such as amino acids and electrolytes), oxygen, carbon dioxide, hormones, and blood cells to and from the cells in the body to provide nourishment and help in fighting diseases, stabilizing temperature and pH, and maintaining homeostasis. Includes the lymphatic system.

VASOCONSTRICTION The narrowing (constriction) of blood vessels by small muscles in their walls. When blood vessels constrict, blood flow is slowed or blocked.

VEDAS The most ancient Hindu scriptures, written in early Sanskrit and containing hymns, philosophy, and guidance on ritual for the priests of Vedic religion and considered to be the foundation of the teachings of both Hinduism and Buddhism.

VO$_2$ MAX The measurement of the maximum amount of oxygen a person can utilize during intense exercise.

WEIL SYNDROME A rare infectious disorder that is a severe form of the bacterial infection caused by Leptospira bacteria known as leptospirosis.

FURTHER READING

BOOKS

Blackburn, Elizabeth, and Elissa Epel. *The Telomere Effect*. New York: Grand Central, 2017.

Bushell, William, Erin Olivio, and Neil Theise. *Longevity, Regeneration, and Optimal Health*. Hoboken, NJ: Wiley-Blackwell, 2009.

Capel, Pierre. *The Emotional DNA: Feelings Don't Exist, They Emerge*. Amsterdam: K.pl Education, 2018. (English translation, 2019.)

Carney, Scott. *What Doesn't Kill Us*. New York: Rodale Books, 2017.

Dale, Cyndi. *The Subtle Body*. Boulder, CO: Sounds True, 2009.

Ehrmann, Wilfried. *Handbuch der Atem-Therapie* (*The Manual of Breath Therapy*). Germany: Param, 2011.

Hof, Wim, and Justin Rosales. *Becoming the Iceman*. Maitland, FL: Mill City Press, 2011.

Hof, Wim, and Koen De Jong. *The Way of the Iceman*. St. Paul, MN: Dragon Door Publications, 2017.

Houtman, Anne, Megan Scudellari, and Cindy Malone. *Biology Now*. New York: W. W. Norton, 2018.

Kamler, Kenneth. *Doctor on Everest*. New York: Lyons Press, 2000.

Kamler, Kenneth. *Surviving the Extremes*. New York: St. Martin's Press, 2004.

Ryan, Christopher. *Civilized to Death*. New York: Simon & Schuster, 2019.

Satchidanada, Sri Swami. *The Yoga Sutras of Patanjali*. Buckingham, VI: Integral Yoga Publications, 2012.

PERIODICALS

Buijze, Geert A., H. M. Y. De Jong, M. Kox, M. G. van de Sande, D. Van Schaardenburg, R. M. Van Vugt, C. D. Popa, P. Pickkers, and D. L. P. Baeten. "An Add-On Training Program Involving Breathing Exercises, Cold Exposure, and Meditation Attenuates Inflammation and Disease Activity in Axial Spondyloarthritis—A Proof of Concept Trial." *PLOS One* 14, no. 12 (December 2, 2019). doi:10.1371/journal.pone.0225749.

Costa, Dora L., Noelle Yetter, and Heather DeSomer. "Intergenerational Transmission of Paternal Trauma Among US Civil War Ex-POWs." *Proceedings of the National Academy of Sciences of the United States of America* 115, no. 44 (October 30, 2018). pnas.org/content/115/44/11215.

Groothuis, Jan T., Thijs M. Eijsvogels, Ralph R. Scholten Scholten, Dick Thijssen, and Maria T. E. Hopman. "Can Meditation Influence the Autonomic Nervous System? A Case Report of a Man Immersed in Crushed Ice for 80 Minutes." innerfire.nl/files/can-meditation-influence-ans-hopman.pdf.

Kandasamy, Narayanan, Sarah N. Garfinkel, Lionel Page, Ben Hardy, Hugo D. Critchley, March Gurnell, and John M. Coats. "Interoceptive Ability Predicts Survival on a London Trading Floor." *Scientific Reports* 6, 32986 (2016). doi: 10.1038/srep32986, nature.com/articles/srep32986.

Kipnis, Jonathan. "Immune System: The Seventh Sense." *Journal of Experimental Medicine* 215, no. 2 (January 16, 2018). rupress.org/jem/article/215/2/397 /42541/Immune-system-The-seventh-sense-Immune-system-Th.e.

Kipnis, Jonathan. "The Seventh Sense." *Scientific American* (August 2018). scientificamerican.com/article/the-seventh-sense/.

Kox, Matthijs, Lucas T. van Eijk, Jelle Zwaag, Joanne van den Wildenberg, Fred C. G. J. Sweep, Johannes G. van der Hoeven, and Peter Pickkers. "Voluntary Activation of the Sympathetic Nervous System and Attenuation of the Innate Immune Response in Humans." *Proceedings of the National Academy of Sciences of the United States of America* 111, no. 20 (May 20, 2014). doi: 10.1073 /pnas.1322174111.

Kozhevnikov, Maria, James Elliott, Jennifer Shephard, and Klaus Gramann. "Neurocognitive and Somatic Components of Temperature Increases During g-Tummo Meditation: Legend and Reality." *PLOS One* 8, no. 3 (March 2013). doi: 10.1371/journal.pone.0058244.

Ledford, Heidi. "Behavioural Training Reduces Inflammation." *Nature News* (May 5, 2014). nature.com/news/behavioural-training-reduces-inflammation-1.15156.

Muzik, Otto, Kaice T. Reilly, and Viabhav Diwadkar. "'Brain Over Body'—A Study on the Willful Regulation of Autonomic Function During Cold Exposure." *NeuroImage* 172 (February 2018). doi: 10.1016/j.neuroimage.2018.01.067.

Nichols, David E. "*N,N*-Dimethyltryptamine and the Pineal Gland: Separating Fact from Myth." *Journal of Psychopharmacology* (November 2, 2017). doi: 10.1177/0269881117736919.

Van Marken Lichtenbelt, Wouter, J. W. Vanhommeirg, N. M. Smudlers, J. M. Drossaerts, G. J. Kemerink, N. D. Bouvy, P. Schrauwen, and G. J. Teule. "Cold-Activated Brown Adipose Tissue in Healthy Men." *New England Journal of Medicine* 360, no. 15 (April 9, 2009). ncbi.nlm.nih.gov/pubmed/19357405.

Vosselman, Maartin J., Guy H. E. J. Vijgen, Boris R. M. Kingma, Boudewijn Brans, and Wouter D. van Marken Lichtenbelt. "Frequent Extreme Cold Exposure and Brown Fat and Cold-Induced Thermogenesis: A Study in a Monozygotic Twin." *PLOS One* 9, no. 7 (July 11, 2014). journals.plos.org /plosone/article?id=10.1371/journal.pone.0101653.

WEBSITES

Angier, Joseph. "Iceman on Everest: 'It Was Easy.'" ABC News (April 14, 2009). abcnews.go.com/Health/story?id=4393377&page=1.

Dattagupta, Shahana. "Arjuna and the Fish Eye: The Fallacy of Being Over-Informed, Hyper-Busy and Multi-Tasking." *Reflections and Revelations* (December 15, 2009). flyingchickadee.wordpress.com/2009/12/15/arjuna-and-the-fish-eye-the-fallacy-of-being-over-informed-hyper-busy-and-multi-tasking/.

Ehrmann, Wilfried. "Intense Breathing and Control of Immune System." wilfried-ehrmann-e.blogspot.com/2015/10/intensive-breathing-has-amazing-effects.html.

Kamler, Kenneth. "World Record Attempt on Regis and Kelly ABC TV Show" (September 17, 2009). wimhofmethod.com/uploads/kcfinder/files/WHM_DataInfo%20Kamler.pdf.

Rogers, Martin. "Extreme Breathing, Cold Helps UFC heavyweight Alistair Overeem Train." *USA Today*, March 1, 2017. usatoday.com/story/sports/ufc/2017/03/01/ufc-209-alistair-overeem-heavyweight/98609304/.

Stanger, Shelby. "Change Your Breath, Change Your Life." *Outside*, June 9, 2016. outsideonline.com/2086911/iceman-cometh.

Steenbeek, Jelle. "Sexual Kung Fu." wimhofmethod.com/blog/sexual-kung-fu. For more information, visit lionwood.nl.

Weatherford, Steve. "How the Wim Hof Experience Has Changed Me." weatherford5.libsyn.com/how-the-wim-hof-experience-has-changed-me.

PHOTOGRAPHY CREDITS

All photography used with permission.
Pages 13 and 85 courtesy of the Hof family archive
Pages 18, 57, and 62 © Henny Boogert
Page 33 © Kersti Niglas
Pages 38, 72, 113, 119, 131, and 168 © Peter Schagen
Video still from *Senior Health Beyond Wellness* on page 101 © NEVCO

ABOUT THE AUTHOR

Wim Hof got the nickname "the Iceman" by breaking a number of world records related to cold exposure. His feats include climbing Mount Kilimanjaro in shorts, running a half marathon above the Arctic Circle on his bare feet, and standing in a container while covered in ice cubes for more than 112 minutes. Having embraced the majestic force of nature, Hof resolved to share his discovery with the rest of the world. He is convinced that everyone can tap into this potential without having to invest decades worth of study, travel, and daring as he has. And so he developed the Wim Hof Method: a natural path to an optimal state of body and mind.

Hof teaches his method in seminars all over the world, but he maintains a spartan training camp in Przesieka, Poland. He resides in Stroe, The Netherlands, with his family. To download the free Wim Hof Method app or enroll in one of our courses, visit wimhofmethod.com.